THE LUCKIEST GIRL IN THE SCHOOL

ANGELA BRAZIL

1st WORLD
LIBRARY
Literary Society

The Luckiest Girl in the School

Angela Brazil

© 1st World Library, 2006
PO Box 2211
Fairfield, IA 52556
www.1stworldlibrary.com
First Edition

LCCN: 2006935172

Softcover ISBN: 1-4218-2464-7
Hardcover ISBN: 1-4218-2364-0
eBook ISBN: 1-4218-2564-3

Purchase *"The Luckiest Girl in the School"*
as a traditional bound book at:
www.1stWorldLibrary.com/purchase.asp?ISBN=1-4218-2464-7

1st World Library is a literary, educational organization
dedicated to:

- Creating a free internet library of downloadable ebooks

- Hosting writing competitions and offering book
publishing scholarships.

Interested in more 1st World Library books?
contact: literacy@1stworldlibrary.com
Check us out at: www.1stworldlibrary.com

1ˢᵗ World Library Literary Society

Giving Back to the World

"If you want to work on the core problem, it's early school literacy."

- James Barksdale, former CEO of Netscape

"No skill is more crucial to the future of a child, or to a democratic and prosperous society, than literacy."

- Los Angeles Times

Literacy... means far more than learning how to read and write... The aim is to transmit... knowledge and promote social participation."

- UNESCO

"Literacy is not a luxury, it is a right and a responsibility. If our world is to meet the challenges of the twenty-first century we must harness the energy and creativity of all our citizens."

- President Bill Clinton

"Parents should be encouraged to read to their children, and teachers should be equipped with all available techniques for teaching literacy, so the varying needs and capacities of individual kids can be taken into account."

- Hugh Mackay

CONTENTS

CHAPTER I

A GREAT CHANGE

"There's no doubt about it, we really must economize somehow!" sighed Mrs. Woodward helplessly, with her house-keeping book in one hand, and her bank pass-book in the other, and an array of bills spread out on the table in front of her. "Children, do you hear what I say? The war will make a great difference to our income, and we can't - simply *can't* - go on living in exactly the old way. The sooner we all realize it the better. I wish I knew where to begin."

"Might knock off going to church, and save the money we give in collections!" suggested Percy flippantly. "It must tot up to quite a decent sum in the course of a year, not to mention pew rent!"

His mother cast a reproachful glance at him.

"Now, Percy, *do* be serious for once! You and Winona are quite old enough to understand business matters. I must discuss them with somebody. As I said before, we shall really have to economize somehow, and the question is where to begin."

"I saw some hints in a magazine the other day," volunteered Winona, hunting among a pile of papers, and fishing up a copy of *The Housewife's Journal*. "Here you are! There's a whole article on War Economies. It says you can halve your expenses if you only try. It gives ten different recipes. Number One, Dispense with Servants. Oh, goody! I don't know how the house would get along without Maggie and Mary! Isn't that rather stiff?"

Class

"It's impossible to be thought of for a moment! I should never dream of dismissing maids who have lived with me for years. I've read that article, and it may be practicable for other people, but certainly not for us. Oh, dear! Some of my friends recommend me to remove to the town, and others say 'Stay where you are, and keep poultry!'"

"We can't leave Highfield! We were all born here!" objected Winona decisively.

"And we tried keeping hens some time ago," said Percy. "They laid on an average three-quarters of an egg a year each, as far as I remember."

"I'm afraid we didn't know how to manage them," replied Mrs. Woodward fretfully. "Percy, leave those papers alone! I didn't tell you to turn them over. You're mixing them all up, tiresome boy! Don't touch them again! It's no use trying to discuss business with you children! I shall write and consult Aunt Harriet. Go away, both of you, now! I want to have a quiet half-hour."

Aunt Harriet stood to the Woodward family somewhat in the light of a Delphic oracle. To apply to her was always the very last resource. Matters must have reached a crisis, Winona thought, if they were obliged to appeal to Aunt Harriet's judgment. She followed Percy into the garden with a sober look on her face.

"You don't think mother would really leave Highfield?" she asked her brother anxiously.

"Bunkum!" replied that light-hearted youth. "We always have more or less of a fuss when my school bills come in. It'll soon

8   Angela Brazil

fizzle out again! Don't you fret yourself. Things will jog on as they always have jogged on. There'll be nothing done, you'll see. Come on and bowl for me, that's a chubby one!"

"But this time mother really seemed to be in earnest," said Winona meditatively, as she helped to put up the stumps.

Mrs. Woodward had been left a widow three years before this story opens. She was a fair, fragile little woman, still pretty, and pathetically helpless. She had been accustomed to lean upon her husband, and now, for lack of firmer support, she leaned upon Winona. Winona was young to act as prop, and though it flattered her sense of importance, it had put a row of wrinkles on her girlish forehead. At fifteen she seemed much older than Percy at sixteen. No one ever dreamt of taking Percy seriously; he was one of those jolly, easy-going, happy-go-lucky, unreliable people who saunter through life with no other aim than to amuse themselves at all costs. To depend upon him was like trusting to a boat without a bottom. Though nominally the eldest, he had little more sense of responsibility than Ernie, the youngest. It was Winona who shouldered the family burdens.

The Woodwards had always lived at Highfield, and in their opinion it was the most desirable residence in the whole of Rytonshire. The house was old enough to be picturesque, but modern enough for comfort. Its quaint gables, mullioned windows and Cromwellian porch were the joy of photographers, while the old-fashioned hall, when the big log fire was lighted, would be hard to beat for coziness. The schoolroom, on the ground floor, had a separate side entrance on to the lawn, leading through a small ante-room where boots and coats and cricket bats and tennis rackets could be kept; the drawing-room had a luxurious ingle nook with cushioned seats, and all the bedrooms but two had a southern aspect. As for the big rambling garden, it was full of delightful old-world flowers that came up year after year: daffodils and violets and snow-flakes, and clumps of pinks, and orange lilies and Canterbury bells, and tall Michaelmas daisies, and ribbon grass and royal Osmunda fern, the sort of flowers that people used to pick in days gone by, put a paper frill round, and call a nosegay or a posy. There was a lawn for tennis and cricket, a pond planted with irises and bulrushes, and a wild corner where crocuses and coltsfoot and golden aconite came up as they liked in the spring time.

Winona loved this garden with somewhat the same attachment that a French peasant bears for the soil upon which he has been reared. She rejoiced in every yard of it. To go away and resign it to others would be tragedy unspeakable. The fear that Aunt Harriet might recommend the family to leave Highfield was sufficient to darken her horizon indefinitely. That her mother had written to consult the oracle she was well aware, for she had been sent to post the letter. She had an instinctive apprehension that the answer would prove a turning-point in her career.

For a day or two everything went on as usual. Mrs. Woodward did not again allude to her difficulties, Percy had conveniently forgotten them, and the younger children were not aware of their existence. Winona lived with a black spot dancing before her mental eyes. It was continually rising up and blotting out the sunshine. On the fourth morning appeared a letter addressed in an old-fashioned slanting handwriting, and bearing the Seaton post mark. Mrs. Woodward read it in silence, and left her toast unfinished. Aunt Harriet's communications generally upset her for the day.

"Come here, Winona," she said agitatedly, after breakfast. "Oh, dear, I wish I knew what to do! It's so very unexpected, but of course it would be a splendid thing for you. If only I could consult somebody! I suppose girls nowadays will have to learn to support themselves, and the war will alter everything, but I'd always meant you to stop at home and look after the little ones for me, and it's very -"

"What does Aunt Harriet say, mother?" interrupted Winona, with a catch in her throat.

Angela Brazil

"She says a great deal, and I dare say she's right. Oh, this terrible war! Things were so different when I was a girl! You might as well read the letter for yourself, as it concerns you. I always think she's hard on Percy, poor lad! I was afraid the children were too noisy the last time she was here, but they wouldn't keep quiet. I'm sure I try to do my best all round, and you know, Winona, how I said Aunt Harriet -"

But Winona was already devouring the letter.

"10 Abbey Close,
      "Seaton,
       "August 26th.

masculine

"MY DEAR FLORITA, - You are quite right to consult me in your difficulties, and are welcome to any advice which I am   able to offer you. I am sorry to hear of your financial embarrassments, but I am not surprised. The present increase in the cost of living, and extra taxation, will make retrenchments necessary to everybody. In the circumstances I should not advise you to leave Highfield. ("Oh, thank goodness!" ejaculated Winona.) The expense of a removal would probably cancel what you would otherwise save. Neither should I recommend you to take Percy from Longworth College and send him daily to be coached by your parish curate. From my knowledge of his character I consider the discipline of a public school to be indispensable if he is to grow into worthy manhood, and sooner than allow the wholesome restraint of his house master to be removed at this critical portion of his life, I will myself defray half the cost f his maintenance for the next two years. *needs male role model*

"Now as regards Winona. I believe she has ability, and it is high time to begin to think seriously what you mean to do with her. In the future women will have to depend upon themselves, and I consider that all girls should be trained to gain their own living. The foundation of every career is a good education - without this it is impossible to build at all, and Winona certainly cannot obtain it if she remains at home. The new High School at Seaton is offering two open Scholarships to girls resident in the County, the examination for which is on September 8th. I propose that Winona enters for this examination, and that if she should be a successful candidate, she should come to live with me during the period of her attendance at the High School. The education is the best possible, there is a prospect of a University Scholarship to be competed for, and every help and encouragement is given to the girls in their choice of a career. With Winona off your hands, I should suggest that you should engage a competent nursery governess to teach the younger children the elements of order and discipline. I would gladly pay her salary on the understanding that I should myself select her.

has financial independent

"Trusting that these proposals may be of some service, and hoping to hear a better account of your health,

"I remain,

"Your affectionate Aunt

    "and Godmother,

    "Harriet Beach."

Winona laid down the letter with an agitated gasp. The proposition almost took her breath away.

"What an idea!" she exclaimed indignantly. "Mother, of course you won't even dream of it for an instant! I'd *hate* to go and live with Aunt Harriet. It's not to be thought of!"

"Well, I don't know, Winona!" wavered Mrs. Woodward. "We must look at it from all sides, and perhaps Aunt Harriet's right, and it really would be for the best. Miss Harmon's a poor teacher, and I'm sure your music, at any rate, is not a credit to her. You played that last piece shockingly out of time. You know you said yourself that you were getting beyond Miss Harmon!"

Whatever impeachments Winona may have brought against her teacher, she was certainly not prepared to admit them now. She rejected the project of the Seaton High School with the utmost energy and determination, bringing into the fray all that force of character which her mother lacked. Poor Mrs. Woodward vacillated feebly - she was generally swayed by whoever was nearest at the moment - and I verily believe Winona's arguments would have prevailed, and the whole scheme would have been abandoned, had not Mr. Joynson opportunely happened to turn up.

Mr. Joynson was a solicitor, and the trustee of Mrs. Woodward's property. He managed most of her business affairs, and some of her private ones as well. She had confidence in his judgment, and she at once thankfully submitted the question of Winona's future to his decision.

"The very thing for her!" he declared. "Do her a world of good to go to a proper school. She's frittering her time away here. Send her to Seaton by all means. What are you to do without her? Nonsense! Nobody's indispensable - especially a girl of fifteen! Pack her off as soon as you can. Doesn't want to go? Oh, she'll sing a different song when once she gets there, you'll see!"

Thus supported by masculine authority, Mrs. Woodward settled the question in the affirmative, and replied to her aunt by return of post.

Naturally such a stupendous event as the exodus of Winona made a sensation in the household.

"Well, of all the rum shows!" exclaimed Percy. "You and Aunt Harriet in double harness! It beats me altogether!"

"It's atrocious!" groaned Winona. "I'm a victim sacrificed for the good of the family. Oh! why couldn't mother have thought of some other way of economizing? I don't want to win scholarships and go in for a career!"

"Buck up! Perhaps you won't win! There'll be others in for the exam., you bet! You'll probably fail, and come whining home like a whipped puppy with its tail between its legs!"

"Indeed I shan't!" flared Winona indignantly. "I've a little more spirit than that, thank you! And why should you imagine I'm going to fail? I suppose I've as much brains as most people!"

"That's right! Upset the pepper-pot! I was only trying to comfort you!" teased Percy. "In my opinion you'll be returned like a bad halfpenny, or one of those articles 'of no use to anybody except the owner.' Aunt Harriet will be cheated of her prey after all!"

"If Win goes away, I shall be the eldest daughter at home," said Letty airily, shaking out her short skirts. "I'll sit at the end of the table, and pour out tea if mother has a headache, and unlock the apple room, and use the best inkpot if I like, and have first innings at the piano."

"You forget about the nursery governess," retorted Winona. "If I go, she comes, and you'll find you've exchanged King Log for King Stork. Oh, very well, just wait and see! It won't be as idyllic as you imagine. I shall be saved the trouble of looking after you, at any rate."

"What I'm trying to ascertain, madam," said Percy blandly, "is whether your ladyship wishes to take up your residence in Seaton or not. With the usual perversity of your sex you pursue a pig policy. When I venture to picture you seated at the board of your venerable aunt, you protest you are a sacrifice; when, on the other hand, I suggest your return to the bosom of your family, you revile me equally."

"You're the most unsympathetic *beast* I've ever met!" declared Winona aggrievedly.

When she analyzed her feelings, however, she was obliged to allow that they were mixed. Though the prospect of settling down at Seaton filled her with dismay, Percy's gibe at her probable failure touched her pride. Winona had always been counted as the clever member of the family. It would be too ignominious to be sent home labeled unfit. She set her teeth and clenched her fists at the bare notion.

"I'll show them all what I can do if I take a thing up!" she resolved.

In the meantime Mrs. Woodward was immersed in the subject of clothing. Every post brought her boxes of patterns, amongst which she hesitated, lost in choice.

"If I knew whether you're really going to stay at Seaton or not, it would make all the difference, Winona," she fluttered. "It's no use buying you these new things if you're only to wear them at home, but I'd make an effort to send you nice to Aunt Harriet's. I know she'll criticize everything you have on. Dear me, I think I'd better risk it! It would be such a nuisance to have to write for the patterns all over again, and how could I get your dresses fitted when you weren't here to be tried on? Miss Jones is at liberty now, and can come for a week's sewing, but she'll probably be busy if I want her later. Now tell me, which do you really think is the prettier of these two shades? I like the fawn, but I believe the material will spot. What have you done with the lace collar Aunt Harriet gave you last Christmas? She's sure to ask about it if you don't wear it!"

Having decided that on the whole she intended to win a scholarship, Winona bluffed off the matter of her departure.

"I've changed my mind, that's all," she announced to her home circle. "It will be a great comfort to me not to hear Mamie scraping away at her violin in the evenings, or Letty strumming at scales. Think what a relief not to be obliged to rout up Dorrie and Godfrey, and haul them off to school every day! I'm tired of setting an example. You needn't snigger!"

The family grinned appreciatively. They understood Winona.

"Don't you worry! I'll set the example when you're gone," Letty assured her. "I'll be as improving as a copy-book. I wish I'd your chance; I'd stand Aunt Harriet for the sake of going to a big High School. Younger sisters never have any luck! Eldests just sweep the board. I don't know where we come in!"

"Don't you fret, young 'un, you'll score later on!" cooed an indulgent voice from the sofa, where Percy sprawled with a book and a bag of walnuts. "Remember that when you're still in all the bliss and sparkle of your teens, Winona'll be a mature and *passee* person of twenty-two. 'That eldest Miss Wood-ward's getting on, you know!' people will say, and somebody'll reply: 'Yes, poor thing!'"

"They won't when I've got a career," retorted Winona, pelting Percy with his own walnut-shells.

"You assured us the other day that you despised such vanities."

"Well, it depends. Perhaps I'll be a lady tram conductor, and punch tickets, or a post-woman, or drive a Government van!"

"If those are careers for girls, bag me for a steeple jack," chirped Dorrie.

It was perhaps a good thing for Winona that such a short interval elapsed between the acceptance of Aunt Harriet's proposal and the date of the scholarship examination. The ten days were very busy ones, for there seemed much to be done in the way of preparation. Miss Jones, the dressmaker, was inst-alled in the nursery with the sewing-machine, and demanded frequent tryings-on, a process Winona hated.

"I shall buy all my clothes ready made when I'm grown up!" she declared.

"They very seldom fit, and have to be altered," returned her mother. "Do stand still, Winona! And I hope you're learning up a few dates and facts for this examination. You ought to be studying every morning. If only Miss Harmon were home, I'd have asked her to coach you. I'm afraid she'll be disappointed at your leaving, but of course she can't expect to keep you for ever. I heard a rumor that she means to give up her school altogether, and go and live with her uncle. I hope it's true, and then I can take the little ones away with an easy conscience. I don't want to treat her badly, poor thing, but I'm sure teaching's not her vocation."

Winona really made a heroic effort to prepare herself for the coming ordeal. She retired to a secluded part of the garden and read over her latest school books. The process landed her in the depths of despondency.

"I'll never remember anything - never!" she mourned to her family. "To try and get all this into my head at once is like bolting a week's meals at a single go! I know a date here and there, and I've a hazy notion of French and Latin verbs, and a general impression of other subjects, but if they ask me for anything definite, such as the battles of the Wars of the Roses, or a list of the products of India, I'm done for!"

"Go in for Post-Impressionism, then," suggested Percy. "Write from a romantic standpoint, and don't condescend to mere facts. Stick in a quotation or two, and a drawing if possible, and make your paper sound eloquent and dramatic and poetical, and all the rest of it. They'll mark you low for accuracy, but put you on ten per cent. for style, you bet! I know a chap who tries it on at the Coll., and it always pays."

"It's worth thinking about, certainly," said Winona, shutting her books with a weary yawn.

CHAPTER II

AN ENTRANCE EXAMINATION

The Seaton High School was a large, handsome brick building exactly opposite the public park. It had only been erected two years ago, so everything about it was absolutely new and up-to-date. It supplied a great need in the rapidly growing city, and indeed offered the best and most go-ahead education to be obtained in the district.

It was the aim of the school to fit girls for various professions and careers; there was a classical and a modern side, a department for domestic economy, and a commercial class for instruction in business details. Art, music, and nature study were well catered for, and manual training was not forgotten. As the school was intended to become in time a center for the county, the Governors had offered two open free scholarships to be competed for by girls resident in other parts of Ryton-shire, hoping by this means to attract pupils from the country places round about.

On the morning of September 8th, precisely at 8.35, Winona presented herself at the school for the scholarship examination. There were twenty other candidates awaiting the ordeal, in various stages of nervousness or sangfroid. Some looked dejected, some confident, and others hid their feelings under a mask of stolidity. Winona joined them shyly. They were all unknown to one another, and so far nobody had plucked up courage to venture a remark. It is horribly depressing to sit on a form staring at twenty taciturn strangers. Winona bore for awhile with the stony silence, then - rather frightened at the sound of her own voice - she announced:

"I suppose we're all going in for this same exam.!" It was a trite commonplace, but it broke the ice. Everybody looked relieved. The atmosphere seemed to clear.

"Yes, we're all going in - that's right enough," replied a ruddy-haired girl in spectacles, "but there are only two scholarships, so nineteen of us are bound to fail - that's logic and mathematics and all the rest of it."

"Whew! A nice cheering prospect. Wish they'd put us out of our misery at once!" groaned a stout girl with a long fair pigtail.

"I'm all upset!" shivered another.

"It's like a game of musical chairs," suggested a fourth. "We're all scrambling for the same thing, and some are bound to be out of it."

The ruddy-haired girl laughed nervously.

"Suppose we've got to take our sporting luck!" she murmured.

"If nineteen are sure to lose, two are sure to win at any rate," said Winona. "That's logic and mathematics and all the rest of it, too!"

"Right you are! That's a more cheering creed! It doesn't do to cry 'Miserere me' too soon!" chirped a jolly-looking dark-eyed girl with a red hair-ribbon. "'Never say die till you're dead,' is my motto!"

"I'm wearing a swastika for a mascot," said a short, pale girl, exhibiting her charm, which hung from a chain round her neck. "I never am lucky, so I thought I'd try what this would do for me for once. I know English history beautifully down to the end of Queen Anne, and no further, and if they set any questions on the Georges I'll be stumped."

"I've learnt Africa, but Asia would floor me!" observed another, looking up from a geography book, in which she was making a last desperate clutch at likely items of knowledge. "I never can remember which side of India Madras is on; I get it hopelessly mixed with Bombay."

"I wish to goodness they'd go ahead and begin," mourned the owner of the red hair-ribbon. "It's this waiting that knocks the spirit out of me. Patience isn't my pet virtue. I call it cruelty to animals to leave us on tenter-hooks."

Almost as if in answer to her pathetic appeal the door opened, and a teacher appeared. In a brisk, business-like manner she marshaled the candidates into line, and conducted them to the door of the head-mistress' study, where one by one they were admitted for a brief private interview. Winona's turn came about the middle of the row.

"Pass in: as quickly as you can, please!" commanded the teacher, motioning her onward.

As Winona entered, she gave one hasty comprehensive glance round the room, taking in a general impression of books, busts and pictures, then focussed her attention on the figure that sat at the desk. It was only at a later date that she grasped any details of Miss Bishop's personality; at that first meeting she realized nothing but the pair of compelling blue eyes that drew her forward like a magnet.

"Your name?"

"Winona Woodward."

"Age?"

Angela Brazil

"Fifteen."

"Residence?"

"Highfield, Ashbourne, near Great Marston."

"How long have you lived in the county of Rytonshire?"

"Ever since I was born."

Miss Bishop hastily ticked off these replies on a page of her ledger, and handed Winona a card.

"This will admit you to the examination room. Remember that instead of putting your name at the head of your papers, you are to write the number given you on your card. Any candidate writing her own name will be disqualified. Next girl!"

It was all over in two minutes. Winona seemed hardly to have entered the room before she was out again.

"Move on, please!" said the teacher, marshaling the little crowd round the door. "Will those who have seen Miss Bishop kindly go along the corridor."

Several girls who had been standing in a knot made a sudden bolt, and pushed their fellows forward. Somebody jogged Winona's elbow. Her card slid from her grasp and fell on to the ground. As she bent in the crush to pick it up, the ruddy-haired girl stooped on a like errand.

"Dropped mine too! Clumsy, isn't it?" she laughed. "Hope we've got our own! What was your number?"

"I hadn't time to look."

"Well, I'm sure mine was eleven, so that's all right. I wish you luck! Won't we just be glad when it's over, rather!"

At the further end of the corridor was a door with a notice pinned on to it. "Examination for County Scholarships." A mistress stood there, and scrutinized each girl's card as she entered, directing her to a seat in the room marked with the corresponding number. Winona walked rather solemnly to the desk labeled 10. The great ordeal was at last about to begin. She wondered what would be the end of it. Little thrills of nervousness seemed running down her back like drops from a shower-bath. Her hands were trembling. With a great effort she pulled herself together.

"It's no use funking!" she thought. "I'll make as good a shot as I can at things, and if I fail - well, I shall have plenty of companions in misfortune, at any rate!"

A pile of foolscap paper with red-ruled margins, a clean sheet of white blotting paper, and a penholder with a new nib lay ready. Each of the other twenty victims was surveying a supply of similar material. On the blackboard was chalked the word "Silence."

In a dead hush the candidates sat and waited. Exactly on the stroke of nine Miss Bishop entered and handed a sheaf of printed questions to the teacher in charge, who distributed them round the room. The subject for the first hour was arithmetic. Winona read over her paper slowly. She felt capable of managing it, all except the last two problem sums, which were outside her experience. She knew it would mainly be a question of accuracy.

"I'll work them each twice if I've only time," she thought, starting at number one.

An hour is after all only made up of sixty minutes, and these seemed to fly with incredible rapidity. The teacher on the platform had sternly reproved a girl guilty of counting aloud in an agitated whisper, threatening instant expulsion for a repetition of such an offense, but with this solitary exception nobody transgressed the rules. All sat quietly absorbed in their work, and an occasional rustle of paper or scratch of a pen were the only sounds audible. At precisely five minutes to ten the deity on the platform sounded a bell, and ordered papers to be put together. She collected them, handed them to another mistress, then without any break proceeded to deal out the questions for the next hour's examination. This was in geography, and here Winona was not on such sure ground. Granted that you are acquainted with certain rules in arithmetic, it is always possible to work out problems, but it needed more knowledge than she possessed to write answers to the riddles that confronted her. She had never heard of "The Iron Gates," could not place Alcona and Altona, was hazy as to the whereabouts of the Mourne Mountains, and utterly unable to draw an accurate map of the Balkan States. She scored a little on Canada, for she had learnt North America last term at Miss Harmon's, but with Australia and New Zealand she was imperfectly acquainted. She wrote away, getting hotter and hotter as she realized her deficiencies, winding up five minutes before the time allotted, in a flushed and decidedly inky condition.

At eleven a short interval was allowed, and the candidates thankfully adjourned. Outside in the corridor they compared notes.

"Well, of all detestable papers this geography one is the limit!" declared an aggrieved voice.

It was the girl who had said that she always mixed Madras and Bombay, and who had studied her text-book up to the last available moment. Apparently her eleventh hour industry had not sufficed to tide her over her difficulties.

"It was catchy in parts," agreed the owner of the swastika, "but I liked one or two questions. I just happened to know them, so I bowled ahead. That's what comes of wearing a mascot!"

"Don't crow too soon!" laughed the girl with the fair pigtail. "Remember, there are four other exams. to follow. Your luck may leave you at any moment."

"Don't mention more exams.! I feel inclined to turn tail and run home!" declared another.

"There's the bell! Don't give us much time, do they? Now for the torture chamber again! Brace your nerves!"

"I wonder if most of them have done better or worse than I have!" thought Winona, as she took her seat once more at No. 10 desk. "A good many were grumbling, but that sandy-haired girl in the spectacles said nothing. No more did the one with the red hair-ribbon. Of course they might be feeling too agonized for words, but on the other hand they might be secretly congratulating themselves."

It was not the moment, however, for speculation as to her neighbors' progress. The next set of questions was being distributed, and she took up her copy eagerly. Her heart fell as she read it over. Her knowledge of English history was not very accurate, and the facts demanded were for the most part exactly those which she could not remember. The dread of failure loomed up large. She could only attempt about half of the questions, and even in these she was not ready with dates. Then suddenly Percy's advice flashed into her mind. "Write from a romantic standpoint, and make your paper sound poetical." It seemed rather a forlorn hope, and she feared it would scarcely satisfy her examiners, but in such a desperate situation anything was worth trying. Winona possessed a certain facility in essay writing. Prose composition had been her favorite lesson at Miss Harmon's. She collected her wits now, and did the very utmost of which she was capable in the matter of style. Choosing question No. 4, "Write a life of Lady Jane Grey," she proceeded to treat the subject in as post-impressionist a manner as possible. The pathetic tragedy of the young Queen had always appealed to her imagination, and she could have had no more congenial a theme upon which to write, if she had been given free choice of all the characters in the history book.

"'Whom the gods love die young,'" she began, and paused. It seemed an excellent opening, if she could only continue in the same strain, but what ought to come next? Her thoughts flew to a painting of Lady Jane Grey, which she had once seen at a loan collection of Tudor portraits. Why should she not describe it? Her pen flew rapidly as she wrote a word-picture of the sweet, pale face, so round and childish in spite of its earnest expression; the smooth yellow hair, the gray eyes bent demurely over the book. Her heroine seemed beginning to live. Now for her surroundings. A year ago Winona had paid a visit to Hampton Court, and her remembrance of its associations was still keen and vivid. She described its old-world garden by the side of the Thames, where the little King Edward VI. must often have roamed with his pretty cousin Jane: the two wonderful ill-starred children, playing for a brief hour in happy unconsciousness of the fate that faced them. What did they talk about, she asked, as they stood on the paved terrace and watched the river hurrying by? Plato, perchance, and his philosophy, or the marvelous geography-book with woodcuts of foreign beasts that had been specially printed for the young king's use. Did they compare notes about their tutors? Jane would certainly hold a brief for her much-loved Mr. Elmer, who, in sharp contrast to her parents' severity, taught her so gently and patiently that she grudged the time which was not spent in his presence. Edward might bemoan the ill-luck of his whipping-boy, who had to bear the floggings which Court etiquette denied to the royal shoulders, and perhaps would declare that when he was grown up, and could make the laws himself, no children should be beaten for badly said lessons, and Jane would agree with him, and then they would pick the red damask roses that Cardinal Wolsey had planted, and walk back under the shadow of the clipped yew hedge to eat cherries and junket in the room that looked out towards the sunset.

Winona had warmed to her work. Her imagination, always her strongest faculty, completely carried her away. She pictured her heroine's life, not from the outside, as historians would chronicle it, a mere string of events and dates, but from the inner view of a girl's standpoint. Did Jane wish to leave her Plato for the bustle of a Court? Did she care for the gay young husband forced upon her by her ambitious parents? Surely for her gentle nature a crown held few allurements. The clouds were gathering thick and fast, and burst in a waterspout of utter ruin. Jane's courage was calm and hopeful as that of Socrates in the dialogues she had loved.

> "... your soul was pure and true,
> The good stars met in your horoscope,
> Made you of spirit, fire and dew."

quoted Winona enthusiastically. Browning always stirred her blood, and threw her into poetical channels. She cast about in her mind for any other appropriate verses.

> "Ah, broken is the golden bowl, the spirit gone for ever,
> Let the bell toll - a saintly soul floats on the Stygian river.
> Come, let the burial rite be read - the funeral song be sung,
> An anthem for the queenliest dead that ever died so young,
> A dirge for her, the doubly dead, in that she died so young."

"So they finished their foul deed, and laid her to rest," wrote Winona, "the earthly part, that is, which perishes, for the true part of her they could not touch. Farewell, sweet innocent soul, of whom the world was not worthy. To you surely may apply Andre de Chenier's tender lines:

> "'Au banquet de la vie a peine commence
> Un instant seulement mes levres out presse
> La coupe en mes mains encore pleine.'

Vale, little Queen! May it be well with thee! Ave atque vale!"

Winona glanced anxiously at the clock as with a hard breath she paused for a moment and laid down her pen. Her theme had taken her so long that she had only ten minutes left for the other questions. There was no romantic side to be expressed in these, so she scribbled away half-heartedly. Her uncertain memory, which had readily supplied quotations from Browning or Edgar Allan Poe, struck altogether when asked for such sordid details as the names of the Cabal ministry, or the history of the Long Parliament. The bell rang, and left her with her paper only half finished. At one o'clock the candidates were given an hour's rest, and a hot lunch was served to them in the dining-hall. At two they returned to their desks, and the examination continued until half-past four. Winona found the questions tolerable. She did fairly, but not at all brilliantly. Her brains were not accustomed to such long-sustained efforts, and as the afternoon wore on, a neuralgic headache began, and sent sharp throbs of pain across her forehead. It was so irksome to write pages of Latin or French verbs; she had to summon all her courage to make herself do it. The last hour seemed an interminable penance.

At half-past four, twenty-one rather dispirited candidates filed from the room.

"Well, thank goodness it's over! I never want to write another word in my life. My hand's stiff with cramp!" exclaimed the girl with the red hair-ribbon to a sympathetic audience in the passage.

"It was awful! I didn't answer half the questions. My swastika isn't worth its salt. I shall give it away!" mourned the owner of the mascot.

"They expected us to know so very much; we should be absolute encyclopaedias if we had all that pat off at our fingers' ends!" sighed the girl with the fair pigtail.

"How did you get on?" Winona asked the ruddy-haired girl, who was wiping her spectacles nervously.

"Oh, I don't know. It's so hard to tell. I answered most of the questions, but of course I can't say whether they're right or wrong. Wasn't the Latin translation just too horrible? I yearned for a dictionary. And some of the French grammar questions were absolute catches!"

"We went on too long," said Winona. "It would have been much better to spread the exam, over two days."

"Do you think so? I'd rather have 'sudden death' myself. It's such a relief to feel it's finished. It would be wretched to have to begin again to-morrow. I hardly slept a wink last night for thinking about it. I'm going to try and forget it now."

Winona nodded good-by to her fellow candidates, and took her leave. How many of them would she see again, she wondered, and which among all the number would have the luck?

"Certainly not myself," she thought ruefully. "I know my papers weren't up to standard. I believe that red-haired girl will be one. She looked clever!"

Winona had spent the preceding night with Aunt Harriet, who offered to keep her until the result of the examination should be published, but the prospect of spending a week of suspense at Abbey Close was so formidable, that she had begged to be allowed to return home, excusing herself on the plea that she would like to be with Percy during the remainder of his holidays. It was a very subdued Winona who reached High-field next afternoon.

"Hello, Tiddleywinks! You've lost the starch out of you!" Percy greeted her. "Did they say they wouldn't have you at any price?"

"The result won't be out till the fifteenth, but I expect I've failed," answered Winona gloomily.

"Buck up, young 'un! Look at yours truly! I fail nine times out of ten, and do I take it to heart?"

Winona laughed in spite of herself. Percy's complacency over small achievements was proverbial. But she had higher ambitions, and the cloud of depression soon settled down again. Her temper, not always her strong point, displayed a degree of irritability that drove her family to the verge of mutiny.

"Really, Winona, I don't remember you so fractious since you were cutting your teeth!" complained her much-tried mother.

The days dragged slowly by. Winona had never before realized that each hour could hold so many minutes. On the morning of the 15th she came down to breakfast with dark rings round her eyes.

"I shall be glad to be put out of my misery!" she thought, as the postman's rap-tap sounded at the door.

Mamie made a rush for the letter-box, and returned bearing a foolscap envelope addressed to:

MISS WINONA WOODWARD,
Highfield,
Ashbourne,
nr. Great Marston.

Winona opened it with trembling fingers. But as she read, her face flushed and her eyes sparkled.

"I have much pleasure in informing you" (so ran the letter) "that the Governors of the Seaton High School have decided to award you a Scholarship tenable for two years...."

In silence she passed the paper to her mother.

"Congratulations, dear child!" cried Mrs. Woodward, clapping her hands. "It's the unexpected that happens!"

"Oh, my goodness!" ejaculated Percy. "You never mean to tell me that Tiddleywinks has actually been and gone and won!"

CHAPTER III

SEATON HIGH SCHOOL

The autumn term at Seaton High School began on September 22nd. On the 21st Winona set forth with great flourish of trumpets, feeling more or less of a heroine. To have been selected for a scholarship among twenty-one candidates was a distinction that even Aunt Harriet would admit. In the brief interval pending her departure, her home circle had treated her with a respect they had never before accorded her.

"I hope you'll do well, child," said her mother, half proud and half tearful when it came to the parting. "We shall miss you here, but when you get on yourself you must help the younger ones. I shall look to you to push them on in life."

There is a certain satisfaction in the knowledge that you are considered the prop of the family. Winona's eyes glowed. In imagination she was already Principal of a large school, and providing posts as assistant mistresses for Letty, Mamie and Doris, that is to say unless she turned her attention to medicine, but in that case she could be head of a Women's Hospital, and have them as house surgeons or dispensers, or something else equally distinguished and profitable. It might even be possible to provide occupation for Godfrey or Ernie, though this was likely to prove a tougher job than placing the girls. With such a brilliant beginning, the future seemed an easy walk-over.

Angela Brazil

Mrs. Woodward was exulting over the fact that she had engaged Miss Jones when she did, and that Winona's school clothes were all made and finished. There had been a fluster at the last, when it was discovered that her mackintosh was fully six inches too short for her new skirts, and that she had outgrown her thick boots, but a hurried visit to Great Marston had remedied these deficiencies, and the box was packed to everybody's satisfaction. There was a universal feeling in the family that such an outfit could not fail to meet with Aunt Harriet's approval. The first sight of the nightdress case and the brush-and-comb bag must wring admiration from her. They had been bought at a bazaar, and were altogether superior to those in daily use. As for the handkerchief case, Letty had decided that unless one equally well embroidered were presented to her on her next birthday, she would be obliged to assert her individuality by showing temper.

Winona walked into the dressing-room of the High School on September 22nd with a mixture of shyness and importance. On the whole the latter predominated. It was a trifle embarrassing to face so many strangers, but it was something to have won a scholarship. She wondered who was the other fortunate candidate.

"I expect it will be that red-haired girl with the spectacles," she thought. "I believe she answered every question, though she was rather quiet about it."

She looked round, but could not see the ruddy locks, nor indeed any of the companions who had taken the examination with her.

"Hunting for some one you know?" asked a girl who had appropriated the next hook to hers.

"Yes, at least I'm not sure whether she'll be here or not. I believe her name's Marjorie Kaye."

"Never heard of her!"

"There are heaps of new girls," volunteered another who stood by.

"I wondered if she'd won a County Scholarship," added Winona.

"Ask me a harder! I tell you I've never heard her name before."

"I've won the other scholarship."

Winona's voice was intended to sound very casual.

"Indeed!"

Her neighbor was taking off her boots, and did not seem as much impressed as the occasion merited.

"Oh! so you're one of the 'outlanders,'" sniggered another. "It's a sort of 'go into the highways and hedges and compel them to come in' business."

"I suppose we shall be having Council School Scholarships next!" drawled a third.

They were friends, and went off together without another glance at Winona. She followed soberly, wondering what she ought to do next. She had a vague idea that the winner of a scholarship should present herself at the Head Mistress' study to receive a few words of encouragement and congratulation on her success. At the top of the stairs she met the mistress who had presided over the examination. The latter greeted her unceremoniously.

"Winona Woodward, you've been placed in V.a., first room to the right, round the corner. You'll find the number on the door."

Other girls were hurrying in the same direction. Winona entered with what seemed to her quite a small crowd.

Angela Brazil

Everybody appeared to know where to go, except herself. She stood in such evident hesitation that one, more good-natured than the rest, remarked:

"You'd better seize on any desk you fancy, as quick as you can. They're getting taken up fast, if you want a front one!"

Winona slid into the nearest seat at hand, and appropriated it by placing her note-book, pencil-box, ruler, atlas and dictionaries inside the desk.

The room was filling quickly. Every moment fresh arrivals hurried in and took their places. Marjorie Kaye was nowhere to be seen, but in the second row sat the dark-eyed girl with the red ribbon in her hair. She turned round and nodded pleasantly.

"So she's got the other scholarship!" thought Winona. "I shouldn't have expected it. I'd have staked my reputation on the sandy-haired one. Well, I suppose her answers weren't correct, after all. I'm rather glad on the whole it's this girl; she looks jolly."

At that moment Miss Huntley, the form mistress, entered and took the call-over, and the day's work began. Each girl was given a time-table and a list of the books she would require, and after that, class succeeded class until one o'clock, with a ten minutes' interval for lunch at eleven. The conclusion of the morning left Winona with a profound respect for High School methods. After the easy-going routine of Miss Harmon's it was like stepping into a new educational world. She supposed she would be able to keep pace with it when she got her books, but the mathematics, at any rate, were much more advanced than what she had before attempted. As she walked down the corridor, the girl with the red hair-ribbon overtook her, and claimed acquaintance.

"So you're Winona Woodward? And I'm Garnet Emerson. We had the luck, after all! I'm sure I never expected to win. It was the greatest surprise to me when the letter arrived. Yes, five of the other candidates are at school, but they've been put in IV.a., and IV.b. Marjorie Kaye? You mean that girl in spectacles? No, she's not come. I heard her say that if she didn't win she was to be sent somewhere else. Where are you staying? With an aunt? I'm with a second cousin. She's nice, but I wish they'd open a hostel; it would be topping to be with a heap of others, wouldn't it? We'd get up acting in the evenings, and all sorts of fun. Well, perhaps that may come later on. I shall see you this afternoon, shan't I?"

"Yes, I'm coming for my books. It's too late to stop and get them now."

Afternoon attendance at the High School was not nominally compulsory. All the principal subjects were taken in the morning, but there were classes for drawing, singing or physical culture from half-past two until four, and practically very few girls had more than one free afternoon in a week. Any who liked might do preparation in their own form room, and many availed themselves of the permission, especially those who came from a distance, and stayed for dinner at the school. When Winona first examined her time-table she had not considered its demands excessively formidable, but before she had been a week at Seaton she began to realize that she would have very few spare moments to call her own. Miss Bishop believed in girls being fully occupied, and in addition to the ordinary form work, expected every one to take part in the games, and in the numerous societies and guilds which had been instituted. Winona found that she was required to join the Debating Club, and the Patriotic Knitting Guild, while a Dramatic Society and a Literary Association would be prepared to open their doors to her if she proved worthy of admission. So far, however, she considered that she had enough on her hands. The demands of her new life were almost over-whelming, and she lived from day to day in a whirl of fresh experiences. It took her some time even to grasp the names of the seventeen other girls in her form. Audrey Redfern, her left-hand neighbor, was friendly, but Olave Parry, at the desk in front, ignored her very existence. She gathered that Audrey, like herself, was a new-comer, while Olave had attended the school since its foundation; but she did not realize the significance of this in the difference of their behavior to her. The fact was that the three new girls in the form were on probation. The others, who had come up from the Lower School, and were well versed in the traditions of the place, were not willing to admit them too quickly into favor. They talked them over in private.

"Audrey Redfern seems a decent enough little soul," said Estelle Harrison. "There's really nothing offensive about her, to my mind. Garnet Emerson I rather like. I fancy she could be jolly. I'm going to speak to her in a day or two, but not too soon."

"What do you think of Winona Woodward?" queried Bessie Kirk.

"Much too big an opinion of herself. Began bragging about her scholarship first thing. She needs sitting upon, to my mind."

"She's pretty!"

"Yes, and she knows it, too!"

"Well, she can't help knowing it. I call her most striking looking. Her eyes are lovely, though I never can make out whether they're dark gray or hazel under those long lashes. Her hair's just the color of bronze, and such a lot of it! It beats Joyce Newton's hollow; besides, Joyce has absolutely white eyelashes."

"Like a pig's!" laughed Hilda Langley. "I agree with you that Winona's pretty, but I don't think she'll ever be a chum of mine, all the same."

The result of the stand-off attitude on the part of the rest of the form was the cementing of a close friendship between

Winona and Garnet. It seemed natural for the holders of the two County Scholarships to become chums, also they found each other's society congenial. It marked a new epoch for Winona. She had had few friends of her own age. She had been the eldest pupil at Miss Harmon's small school, and her sisters were so much younger than herself that their interests were on a different plane to her own. Garnet, with her merry brown eyes, eager and enthusiastic nature, and amusing tongue, seemed a revelation.

The two girls spent every available moment together, and soon waxed confidential on the subject of their home affairs.

"We're all named after precious stones," said Garnet. "Pearl, my eldest sister, is classics mistress at a school; Jacinthe is studying for a health visitor, Ruby is at a Horticultural College, and Beryl is secretary at a Settlement. Aren't there a lot of us? All girls too, and not a single brother. I'm the baby of the family! I'd like to go to Holloway, if I can get a scholarship, but that remains to be seen. Meanwhile two years at the High's not so bad, is it? I expect I'm going to enjoy it. Aren't you?"

"Yes - perhaps. If the rest of the form were nicer, I might."

"Oh, they'll come round! We can't expect them to take us to their bosoms straight off! We're goods on approval."

"We've as much right here as they have!" grunted Winona.

"But they were here first, and of course that always counts for something. We shall have to show that we're worth our salt before we get any footing in the form. The question is how best to do it."

Winona shook her head. It was beyond her comprehension.

"I had a few tips from Jacinthe," ruminated Garnet. "She was Captain the last year she was at school, so she ought to know.

You see, we've to steer between Scylla and Charybdis. We mustn't push ourselves forward too violently, or they'll call us cheeky, but on the other hand, if we're content to take a back seat, we may stay there for the rest of the term. Comprenez vous? It's a matter of seizing one's chance. I've an idea floating about in my mind. Do you happen to be anything extra special at singing, or reciting, or acting?"

"I haven't had much practice at acting, but I can play the guitar. Mummie taught me. She lived in Spain for three years when she was a girl, and learnt there."

"The very thing! How perfectly splendid! I play the mandoline myself, and the two go so well together. Did you bring your guitar with you?"

"No. I didn't think I should have any time for it."

"But you could write for it, couldn't you?"

"Oh, yes! Mummie would send it to me."

"Well, this is my idea. You know next week there's to be a big general meeting of the whole school to choose a Games Captain. So far the games department here is rather in its infancy. I've been making enquiries, and there isn't such a thing as a form trophy. There certainly ought to be, to spur on enthusiasm. I'm going to pluck up my courage, tackle one or two members of the Sixth, and suggest that after the meeting we hold a sing-song, and take a collection to provide a form trophy. I don't believe anybody's ever thought of it."

"Ripping! But what exactly is a sing-song?"

"Oh, just an informal concert. I thought if you and I played the mandoline and guitar together, it would make a good item. I see two of the prefects coming along over there, I believe I'll go and ask them."

"I admire your courage!"

Garnet returned in a few minutes, tolerably well satisfied with her mission.

"I believe the idea will catch on," she announced. "Of course I couldn't expect them to say 'yes' immediately. They were very cautious, and said they would put it to the form. I've sown the seed at any rate, and we must wait for developments."

Apparently Garnet's proposition proved acceptable to the Sixth, for the very next day a notice was pinned on the board in the hall:

> "There will be a General Meeting of the School on Tuesday, October 4th, at 3 p.m., for the purpose of electing a Games   Captain.
>
> "The meeting will be followed by a Symposium, when a collection will be taken, the proceeds of which will be devoted to the purchase of a form trophy.
>
> "Performers kindly submit their names without delay to M. HOWELL, as the program is being made up."

Garnet was one of the first to read the notice, and she started off at once to the Sixth Form room. She sought out Winona on her return.

"So my little scheme's come off!" she beamed. "You bet the Sixth will take all the credit for evolving it, but I don't care! I've put our names down for a mandoline and guitar duet, and said we'd be ready to help with any accompaniments they like. Meg Howell just jumped at that. It seems Patricia Marshall and Clarice Nixon are going to sing a Christy Minstrel song, and she thought our instruments would add to the effect no end. I tell you we shall score. Did you write for your guitar?"

"Yes, I expect it will be sent off to-day."

"Then we must begin and practice. I've got a topping duet that's quite easy. Can you come home with me after school to-morrow for half an hour or so? I know my cousins will be glad to see you. Then we might try over one or two things, and see how they go."

"It will be all right if I tell Aunt Harriet I shall be late," agreed Winona.

The instrument arrived the same evening, so she was able to keep her promise to Garnet next day. Fortunately they had only one class that afternoon, and were able to leave school at half-past three. Garnet's cousins lived within a short tramcar ride. They were musical people, and sympathized with her project. Garnet led Winona into the drawing-room, and began without waste of time.

"Let me look at your guitar! Oh, what a beauty! What's the label inside? Juan Da Costa, Seville! Then it must be Spanish. I suppose they're the best. My mandoline's Italian; it was made in Milan. We must tune them together, mustn't we? Can you read well? This is the book of duets. I thought this Barcarolle would be easy, it has such a lovely swing about it. Here's the guitar part."

CHAPTER IV

THE SYMPOSIUM

By the aid of diligent practicing in private, and several rehearsals at Garnet's house, the girls at last got their duet to run smoothly. Garnet was frankly pleased.

"The two instruments go so nicely together! A mandoline's ever so much better played with a guitar accompaniment than with the piano. I say, suppose we were to get an encore!"

"I don't suppose anything of the sort."

"Don't be too modest. It's as well to be prepared."

"I'm not going to practice anything more, so I warn you."

"Well, take something you know, from your own book. This song. I could play the air very softly on the mandoline, and we'd both sing it. That won't give you any extra trouble."

"It isn't the trouble so much as the state of my fingers. They're getting sore. If I let a blister come, I shan't be able to play at all."

"Then for goodness' sake don't play any more to-day, and soak your fingers in alum when you get home."

The general meeting on Tuesday was a very important event,

for it marked the opening of the winter session of games and guilds. During the first week or ten days of the autumn term the girls had enough to do in settling into the work of their new forms, but now October was come everybody began to think about hockey, and to consider the advisability of beginning rehearsals for various Christmas performances.

"I always hate the end of September," proclaimed Grace Olliver. "It's so fine, and the geraniums are still so fresh in the park, that you're deceived into thinking it's still summer, yet when you try to play tennis, you find the courts horrible, and you cut up the grass in half an hour. I'm glad when the leaves all come off, and you know it's autumn, and you look up your hockey jersey, and think what sport you had last winter over 'The Dramatic.' I'm fond enough of cricket, but I'd really rather have winter than summer. On the whole, there's more going on."

"I'm glad Margaret Howell's head of the school," replied Evelyn Richards. "She's A1 at all the guilds, though I don't think she's much chance of being elected Games Captain."

"All the better. It's quite enough for Margaret to act head. She's good enough at that, I admit. Makes an ideal president. But a girl who's literary isn't generally sporty as well. It stands to reason she can't do both properly."

"Meg doesn't want to be Games Captain; it's not in her line," volunteered Beatrice, Margaret's younger sister. "She told me to tell you all to vote for Kirsty Paterson."

"Kirsty's topping!"

"What's this Symposium we're to have after the meeting?" asked Grace.

"Why, I don't exactly know," laughed Evelyn. "I looked 'symposium' up in the dictionary, and it said: 'literally a drinking together; a merry feast; a convivial party.' I don't know what we're going to drink, unless we bring lemon kali and pass it round, like they used to do the loving cup in the Middle Ages!"

"I suppose it'll be just a kind of concert. But how about the collection? What are we supposed to give?"

"Anything you like, from a penny upwards," replied Beatrice. "Meg calculated that two hundred and six pennies would be seventeen and twopence, and some girls will probably give more, so she thinks we're sure of a sovereign, and that ought to buy a decent trophy, something to begin upon, at any rate. One must make a start."

"Right you are! A penny won't break the banks of even the First Form babes, and millionaires can give their half-crowns, if they're so disposed!"

Punctually at 3 p.m. on the following Tuesday, the whole school assembled in the gymnasium. No mistress was present, for on occasions such as this Miss Bishop believed in self-government. She could trust her head girl and prefects, and had armed them with full authority. Winona anticipated the meeting with excitement and curiosity. It was altogether outside her experience. She had never in her life attended such a function. Garnet, whose elder sisters had been at large schools, had sketched an outline of what was likely to take place, but even Garnet's information was second-hand. Though she had now been exactly a fortnight at Seaton, Winona still felt more or less of a new-comer. She had hardly spoken to any one outside her own form, and knew the names of comparatively few of her two hundred and five school-fellows. Without Garnet she would have been quite at a loss how to steer her course in this great ocean of school life; she thankfully accepted her friend as pilot, and for the present was content to follow her lead. The two girls presented themselves in the gymnasium in good time, and took their seats among the other members of V.a. The front bench was occupied by a row of ten-year-olds who had come up this term from the

Preparatory, and who sat squeezing each others' arms, highly impressed with the importance of their remove. Behind them Form II., a giggling crew rather more *au fait* with the ways of the school, effervesced occasionally into excited squeals, and were instantly suppressed by a prefect. The Third and Fourth, which comprised the bulk of the girls from twelve to fifteen, occupied the middle of the hall, a lively, self-confident and rather obstreperous set, all at that awkward age which is anxious to claim privileges, but not particularly ready to submit to the authorized code. Every one of them was talking at the extreme pitch of her voice, and the noise was considerable. Patricia Marshall and Clarice Nixon looked at each other and frowned ominously, but as the hands of the big clock pointed almost to three, they judged it better not to interfere, and the din continued.

At the stroke of the hour, Margaret Howell strode on to the platform. She was a tall, fine-looking girl of seventeen, with bright hazel eyes, regular features, and a thick brown plait that fell below her waist. Her ready powers of speech, clear ringing voice, brisk decisive tone, and a certain personal magnetism showed her to be that *rara avis*, a born leader. It was fortunate indeed for the school that its headship this year should have fallen to Margaret. The need for a firm but judicious hand on the reins was great. During the two previous years of the school's existence the self-government had been in a state of evolution. For the first year, when everybody was new together, comparatively little could be done. The school must find itself before it began to form its private code of laws. In the second year ill-luck had raised to the post of honor Ivy Chatterton, a clever but most untactful girl, whose quick temper had brought her into constant collision with her prefects. Many were the squalls which had swept over the school, of so serious a nature sometimes as almost to wreck several of the guilds. The younger girls, following the example of their elders, had quarreled hotly, and indulged in an incredible amount of petty spite, and altogether the current tone had been anything but desirable. Miss Bishop, who had seen, to her sorrow, this downward trend, had welcomed the advent of Margaret, believing her to have the ability to cope with difficult situations, and at the same time to have the grit and self-control not to allow her head to be turned by her elevation to office.

"You will have a great responsibility: I am giving you unusual power, and I trust that you will make the highest use of it," she had said to the girl, during a certain quiet ten minutes' talk in her study, and Margaret had held herself very straight, and had answered: "I'll do my level best, Miss Bishop!"

All eyes were now fixed on the head girl as she stood in the center of the platform, ringing the bell for silence. The clamor subsided as if by magic, and in the midst of a dead hush she began her speech.

"Girls! We've been back now for a whole fortnight - time for most of us to shake down into our places, isn't it? The school year's fairly started, and we've met together this afternoon to talk about a number of things that are of very great importance to us all. You all know that a school - to be worth anything - has two sides. There's the inside part, with classes and prep. and exams. - what's generally called the 'curriculum' - that's managed by the mistresses. And there's the outside part, the games and sports and concerts and guilds - that's run by the girls themselves. Now I think, if we arrange well, we ought to be able to look forward to three very jolly terms. Everything depends upon making a good start. I've been getting to know how they manage in several other big schools, and I propose that we frame our code by theirs. What we want first of all is a feeling of unity and public spirit. Each girl must make up her mind to do all she can to push on the 'Seaton High.' We want to win matches, and have a good sports record, and generally build up a reputation. Slacking at games must be out of the question. Everybody must buck up all round. Those who aren't playing themselves can show their interest by attending the matches. It makes the greatest difference to an eleven to know that their own side is watching their play, and ready to cheer them on. There's nothing so forlorn and depressing as to see whole rows of the enemy's school hats on the spectators' benches, and only half-a-dozen of one's own - yet that's what happened when we played Harbury last spring. No wonder we lost! I'm going to ask you presently to elect a Games Captain, and then I want you to support her loyally for the whole of the year. Let her feel that she can depend upon you, and that instead of getting together scratch teams, her difficulty will be how to choose among so many crack players. But as you know, games are not the whole of our business to-day. We have our guilds to consider as well. I want to put these upon a good and firm basis. Last winter we didn't quite know where we were with them, did we? At present we have 'The Dramatic Society,' 'The Debating Club,' 'The Literary Association,' and 'The Patriotic Knitting Guild.' We might very well add a 'Photographic Union' and a 'Natural History League.' They ought all to be run on the same lines. Each must have a President, a Secretary, and a Committee of eight members, who will undertake the business of the Society, and settle all its events. Any difficulty or dispute must be referred to the Prefects' meeting, the decision of which shall be final. Each guild must draw up a list of its own rules; these must be submitted first to the Prefects, then, if passed as satisfactory, they must be written in the minutes book, and strictly adhered to. I want you all to realize that this school is still in its infancy. It's a baby of only two years! But a very promising baby! It's we who are going to make its history. So far we can't say it has had any annals; in the future it must show a whole splendid list of achievements and successes. Years afterwards, when it's the most famous school in the county, we shall be proud to have had the privilege of taking our share in pushing it on, and our names may be handed down to long generations of girls as those who founded its best traditions."

Margaret paused, quite out of breath with her long speech. A storm of applause rose from the audience; the girls clapped and stamped, a few even cheered. Margaret had touched the right string. The idea of making school history appealed to them, and they were ready to respond with enthusiasm to her appeal. Even the ten-year-olds were eager to show their zeal. Winona had never taken her eyes off the speaker. It was a new gospel to her that she was one of the great community, bound to help the common weal. The realization of it stirred her spirit; her imagination danced ahead, and performed prodigies. Suppose she could do something wonderful for the school, and leave her name as a memory to others? The vision gleamed golden. It would be worth living to accomplish that.

"Not half a bad speech!" murmured Garnet approvingly by her side.

Winona started, and came back from the clouds.

"I think it's - just immense!" she answered with a long sigh of admiration.

Margaret was again ringing the bell for silence.

"I'm glad to find you all agree with me," she announced. "Now I want us to get solidly to business, and elect a Games Captain. You remember I asked each to nominate a candidate, and I find that more than two-thirds have handed in the same name - that of Kirsty Paterson. I therefore put Kirsty up for election. It's only fair that I should first go over her qualifications for the office. She was our best center forward last year at hockey, and our best bowler at cricket. She's a thoroughly steady and reliable player herself, and - this is most important - she's able to train others. You know from experience that she's fair and just, and she's tremendously keen. I feel sure that in her hands the games would prosper, and we'd soon show some improvement. Will all those in favor of electing Kirsty kindly stand up?"

There was such a general rising among the girls that most presidents would have considered the matter settled. Margaret, however, liked to do things strictly in order.

"Thanks I Will you please sit down again. Now those against the election kindly stand."

A certain section in the school had intended to vote against Kirsty, but when they saw themselves so enormously outnumbered, they changed their minds. To belong to a minority often means to be unpopular, and it is wise to go with the stream. After all, Kirsty was a thoroughly eligible and desirable candidate. So though a few neighbors elbowed each other, nobody rose.

Margaret waited a moment.

"Do I understand that you're all in favor? Then the motion is carried unanimously. I'm very glad, for I think Kirsty will make an ideal captain. Let's give three cheers for her. Are you ready? Hip-hip-hip hooray!"

The girls responded with full lung power. Some even began to sing: "For she's a jolly good fellow!" and there was a general outcry of "Speech! Speech!" The blushing Kirsty - a bonny, rosy, athletic looking lassie - was seized by her fellow prefects, and dragged, in spite of her protests, to the front of the platform. Kirsty had been born north of the Tweed, and in moments of excitement her pretty Scottish burr asserted itself.

"It's verra kind of you to elect me," she began. "I'm afraid I'm no hand at making speeches. I preferr deeds to worrds. We'll all put ourr shoulderrs to the wheel, and win forr the school, won't we? I hope we'll have a splendid yearr!"

At that she retired amidst rapturous applause. Margaret again rang the bell for silence, and proceeded with the business of the meeting, which was to elect the officers for the various societies and guilds. This being satisfactorily settled, she turned to affairs of lighter moment.

"I'm sure you'll all agree that it is very desirable for us to have a form trophy, for hockey, at any rate. Perhaps by next summer we'll get one for cricket as well. It will spur us on to have a little wholesome competition amongst ourselves. As I announced on the notice board, we are now going to give a short entertainment, at the close of which a collection will be taken for the object I have just mentioned. I hate begging, so give what you like, but of course it depends on your generosity this afternoon what kind of a trophy we are able to buy. The first item on our program is a piano solo by Hester King."

Hester was one of the best music pupils in the school. She had a good crisp touch and considerable execution, and led off the concert with a sprightly tarantella. A violin solo followed, by Sibyl Lee, a member of V.b., who was rather nervous, but acquitted herself fairly well on the whole.

"I thought I'd break down," she confided to her friends. "The sight of all those eyes staring at me quite put me off. I don't wonder blind musicians are generally successes, they can't see the audience. Well, never mind, I've done my bit, at any rate!"

The next on the list was a song from Annie Hardy. She had chosen "Keep the Home Fires Burning," and rendered it with great effect, the whole room joining with enthusiasm in the chorus. It took so well that there were shouts of "Encore!" and Annie came back smiling to give "Khaki Boys," which roused her audience to an even higher pitch of patriotic fervor. A recitation, "Our Hockey Match," by Agnes Heath, was felt to be particularly appropriate to the occasion. It was a very good "school piece," humorous as well as exciting, and Agnes had enough dramatic ability to do justice to it. Her own form in particular stamped lustily. The prefects motioned her forward again, but she shook her head. The clapping redoubled. Agnes, escorted to the front by Margaret, bowed and announced:

"Fearfully sorry not to oblige, but this is absolutely the only thing I know, and it's too long to say all over again!"

There was a general laugh, and the audience settled itself to enjoy the next item on the program. Margaret was signaling to Winona and Garnet, and the pair slipped from their places, and made their way to the platform.

"I'm all upset! I hope I shan't break down!" whispered Winona.

"Nonsense! A duet's not so bad as a solo. You'll get on all right. Do for goodness' sake brace up!" implored Garnet. "If you muddle your accompaniment you'll spoil my part. You'll surely never go and fail me!"

The instruments had been put under the piano. Patricia Marshall handed them forth, and sounded the notes for them to be tuned. Clarice Nixon was placing chairs and music-stands. Garnet was tolerably composed, but Winona was suffering from a bad attack of that most unpleasant malady "stage fright." She would have given worlds for a trapdoor in the platform to open, and allow her to subside out of sight. No such convenient arrangement, however, had been provided for the use of bashful performers, the planks were solid, and guaranteed not to give way under any circumstances. There was nothing for it but to take her seat in full view of the audience. There were slightly over two hundred girls in the room, but to Winona's fevered imagination there appeared to be thousands. She wondered how she could ever have had the folly to place herself in such a public situation. Garnet was sounding a few notes and looking at her to begin. For one dreadful moment the room whirled. Perhaps Margaret saw and understood; she laid her hand on Winona's shaking arm, and whispered encouragingly:

"Go on! Don't mind the audience. Just remember that you're playing for the form trophy!"

A sudden revulsion of feeling swept over Winona. All the school patriotism aroused within her by Margaret's speech surged up to meet the crisis. She was no longer an isolated atom, a girl fresh from home, and on trial before the critical eyes of her new form, but a unit in the great life of the school, bound to play her part for the good of the whole, and specially pledged not to fail Garnet in this emergency. Self faded in the larger vision. The color flooded back into her face. She made a desperate effort, and struck the opening chords.

As her friend had reminded her, a duet was quite a different matter from a solo. Directly the mandoline part began, her confidence returned. She tried to think that she was only playing an accompaniment for Garnet. The piece was not difficult, it was in D, quite the easiest key for the guitar, with very few accidentals or high positions. She took courage, and struck her strings crisply, so that the tone rang out well. Her instrument was a good one, very true and mellow, and her mother had taught her the liquid Spanish touch which showed it to its best advantage. Garnet also was doing her best. Her plectrum vibrated evenly and rapidly, and the metallic twang, her gravest fault, was not nearly so evident as usual. The audience, unfamiliar with these particular instruments, was not hypercritical, and so long as the players kept well together, and sounded no discords, their skill was judged to be excellent. The Barcarolle had an attractive swing about it, and a romantic suggestion of gondolas and lapping water and moonlight serenades. As the last notes of the air on the mandoline died away, Winona swept her thumb over the strings of her guitar in a tremendous final chord. It had quite a magnificent and professional effect. There was no mistake about the applause; it was simply clamorous.

"Stand up and bow!" whispered Margaret, nudging the unaccustomed performers. "That's right! Bow again! It's most clearly an encore. Have you brought anything else with you? Good biz! Don't waste any more time, then. We're rather late."

The song that Winona had chosen was a bright little Irish ditty, with a catchy tune and lively accompaniment. Garnet played the air softly on the mandoline, and the two girls sang in unison, keeping strictly together, and pronouncing very plainly, so that the point of the amusing words should not be lost. The audience shrieked with laughter, and would have demanded a further encore, had not Margaret pointed to the clock, and shaken her head firmly. There were other items on

Angela Brazil

the program and time was going all too fast.

Another violin solo, a recitation and a Highland fling followed; then the concert wound up with a Christy Minstrel song from several members of the Sixth. This last was the triumph of the afternoon. Patricia prided herself on her preparations. She had placed a newspaper inside the grand piano over the strings, and when the hammers struck against it the effect of the accompaniment was exactly that of a banjo. She had borrowed two sets of castanets, a pair of cymbals, and a triangle, and with these loud-sounding instruments she and her companions emphasized the chorus. Garnet and Winona helped with mandoline and guitar, so the general result was quite orchestral. During the performance of this chef-d'oeuvre some of the prefects went round with collecting bags, which were passed along the benches.

"Come, my dark-eyed honey,
And help to spend my money,"

chanted the minstrels lustily, and the audience smiled at the appropriateness of the words.

It was felt that the Symposium had been an enormous success. The girls were quite loath to leave, and dispersed slowly from the gymnasium. Many eyes were turned on Winona and Garnet as they carried their instruments down from the platform. "Who are they?" every one was asking, for so far their names were not known outside their own form. "The two County Scholarship holders," somebody replied, and the information was passed on.

Next morning, Margaret proudly posted up the result of the collection, which amounted to L2 13s. 7d. - a very substantial sum in the estimation of the school.

"It ought to be sufficient to buy a cup!" she triumphed. "Miss Bishop has promised to send for some catalogues, so that we can look up the prices. We shall start the season well, at any rate. Kirsty's almost ready to stand on her head! I never saw any one so elated!"

"Except yourself!" smiled Patricia.

"Cela va sans dire, camarade!"

Garnet and Winona, walking down the High Street together after the performance, also compared notes.

"It was fine! I do admire Margaret. Mustn't it be splendid to be head of the school?" sighed Garnet enviously.

"Do you think so? Yes, I suppose it is, but if I had my choice, I'd a dozen times over rather be Games Captain," answered Winona.

CHAPTER V

AUNT HARRIET — masculine

It is high time now that we paused to consider a very important person indeed in this story, namely Miss Harriet Beach, but for whose invitation Winona would never have attended Seaton High School at all. Aunt Harriet was what is generally known as "a character," that is to say, she was possessed of a strong personality, and was decidedly eccentric. Though her age verged on sixty she preserved the energy of her thirties, and prided herself upon her physical fitness. She was tall, with a high color, keen brown eyes, a large nose, a determined mouth, and iron gray hair. In her youth she must have been handsome, and even now her erect figure and dark, well-marked eyebrows gave her a certain air of distinction. She was a most thoroughly capable woman, reliable, and strongly philanthropic: not in a sentimental way, however; she disapproved of indiscriminate almsgiving, and would have considered it a crime to bestow a penny on a beggar without making a proper investigation of his case. She was a tower of strength to most of the charitable institutions in the city, a terror to the professional pauper, but a real friend to the deserving. Her time was much occupied with committees, secretarial duties, district visiting, workhouse inspection and other public interests. She was apt indeed to have more than her share of civic business; her reputation for absolute reliability caused people to get into the habit of saying "Oh, go to Miss Beach!" on every occasion, and as she invariably proved the willing horse, she justified the proverb and received the work in increased proportions.

Like most people, Aunt Harriet had her faults. She was apt to be a trifle overbearing and domineering, she lacked patience with others' weaknesses, and was too doctrinaire in her views. She tried very hard to push the world along, but she forgot sometimes that "the mills of God grind slowly," and that it is only after much waiting and many days that the bread cast upon the waters returns to us. She prided herself on her candor and lack of "humbug." Unfortunately, people who "speak their minds" generally treat their hearers to a sample of their worst instead of their best, and their excessive truthfulness scarcely meets with the gratitude they consider it deserves. Miss Beach's many estimable qualities, however, overbalanced her crudities, her friends shrugged their shoulders and told each other it was "her way," "her heart was all right." Though she might give offense, people forgot it, and came to her again next time they wanted anything done, and the universal verdict was that she was "trying at times," but on the whole one of the most useful citizens which Seaton possessed.

If there was one person more than another who wore out Miss Beach's patience it was her niece and goddaughter, Mrs. Woodward. She had a sincere affection for her, but their two personalities were at absolutely opposite poles. She admitted that Florita was amiable, well-meaning, and thoroughly affectionate, but for the rest she considered her weak, foolishly helpless, liable to extravagance, a poor housekeeper, and a perfect jelly-fish in her methods of bringing up her family. In vain did Aunt Harriet, on successive visits, preach firmness, order, consistency and other maternal virtues; her niece would brace herself up to a temporary effort, but would relax again directly her guest had departed, and the children - little rogues! - discovered at a remarkably early age that they could do pretty much as they liked. The Woodwards always dreaded the advent of Aunt Harriet, her disapproval of their general conduct was so manifest. By dint of urging from their mother they made extra attempts at good behavior before the august visitor, but they were subject to awful relapses. Mrs.

Woodward, on her side, considered she had her trials, for her aunt had a habit of arriving suddenly, giving only a few hours' notice by telegram, and she could not forbear the suspicion that her revered godparent wished to surprise her housekeeping and catch her unprepared. On one occasion, indeed, when the family came down - rather late - for breakfast, Aunt Harriet was discovered sitting on the rustic seat outside the dining-room window. She explained that she had taken the 5 a.m. workmen's train and had come to spend a long day with them, but not wishing to disturb the house at too early an hour she had remained in the garden enjoying the view until somebody arrived downstairs. In spite of her rather angular attitude, Miss Beach was a very kind and generous friend to her widowed niece, and she was the one person in the world to whom Mrs. Woodward naturally thought of turning in time of trouble. Aunt Harriet's advice might not always be palatable, but it was combined with such practical help that there seemed no alternative but to follow it.

Miss Beach, though not a rich woman, was possessed of very comfortable private means. She lived in an old-fashioned house just opposite the Abbey, and her windows looked out on a view of towers and cloisters and tall lime trees, with a foreground of monuments. To some people the array of tomb-stones would have proved a dismal prospect, but she declared it never distressed her in the least. She prided herself greatly on the fact that she had been born in the house where her father, grandfather and great-grandfather had also come into the world and spent their lives. Except for an occasional expedition to Highfield, she rarely left home. All her interests were in Seaton, and she became miserable directly if she were away from her native city.

The little Woodwards had never regarded it as much of a treat to go and stay at 10, Abbey Close. The restraint which the visit necessitated quite neutralized the afternoon at the cinema with which their aunt invariably entertained them. The fine old Chippendale furniture had to be treated with a respect not meted out to the chairs and tables at home, boots must be *being taught how to run a proper house*

scrupulously wiped on the door-mat, bedrooms left tidy, and books and ornaments were to be held altogether sacred from the ravages of prying young fingers.

Winona had taken up her residence there with somewhat the feeling of a novice entering a nunnery. She was not quite sure how she and Aunt Harriet were going to get on. To her great relief, however, things turned out better than she expected. Miss Beach received her with unusual complacency, and the two settled down quite harmoniously together. The fact was that Winona, a visitor with nothing to do, and Winona a busy High School girl, were utterly different persons. It is one thing to wander round somebody else's house and feel bored, and quite another to hang up your hat, realize you are part and parcel of the establishment, and occupy yourself with your own business. Once she had fallen into the swing of work at school Winona began to appreciate the orderliness of her aunt's arrangements. It had never seemed to matter at home if the breakfast were late and she arrived at Miss Harmon's when the clock had struck nine, but at "The High" it was an affair of vital importance to be in her seat before call-over, and she daily blessed the punctuality of Aunt Harriet's cook. It was also a great boon to be able to prepare her lessons in quiet. Her family had never realized the necessity of silence during study hours, and she had been used to learn French vocabularies or translate her Latin exercises to a distracting accompaniment of Ernie's trumpet, Dorrie's and Mamie's quarrels, Godfrey's mouth organ, and Letty's strumming upon the piano.

"It would have been utterly impossible to do my prep. at home!" she thought sometimes. "I'd no idea what work was like before I came to Seaton 'High'! It would do those youngsters good to have a drilling! I wish they could have been in the Preparatory. No, I don't! Because then I should have had them here, and it would have been good-by to all peace. On the whole things are much better as they are."

Miss Beach was so extremely busy with her own multifarious occupations that she had not time to see very much of her great-niece. She made every arrangement for her comfort, however, and caused the piano to be moved into the dining-room for the convenience of her practicing. She had always had a tender spot for Winona, whom she regarded as the one hopeful character in a family of noodles. She talked to her at meal times about a variety of subjects, some of them within her intelligence, but others completely - so far - above her head. She even tried to draw her out upon school matters. This, however, was a dead failure. Winona, most unfortunately, could not overcome her awe for her aunt, and refused to expand. To all the questions about her Form, her companions, teachers, lessons or new experiences, she replied in monosyllables. It was a sad pity, for Miss Beach had really hoped to win the girl's confidence and prove a temporary mother to her, but finding her advances repulsed she also shrank back into her shell, and the intimacy which might have existed between them was postponed to future years. Young folks often fail to realize what an interest their doings may have to grown-up people, and how their bright fresh outlook on life may come as a tonic to older and wearier minds. It never struck Winona to try to amuse or entertain her aunt. At her present crude stage of development she was incapable of appreciating the subtle pathos that clings round elderly lives, and their wistful longing to be included in the experiences of the rising generation. Shyness and lack of perception held her silent, and the empty corner in Aunt Harriet's heart went unfilled. — because childless

Saturday and Sunday were the only days upon which Winona had time to feel homesick. Her mother had at first suggested her returning to Highfield for the week ends, but Miss Beach had strongly vetoed the project on the justifiable ground that even the earliest train from Ashbourne on Monday mornings did not reach Seaton till 9.30, so that Winona would lose the first hour's lesson of her school week. She might have added that she considered such frequent home visits would prove highly unsettling and interfere greatly with her work, but for once she refrained from stating her frank opinion, probably deeming the other argument sufficient, and willing to spare Mrs. Woodward's feelings.

Letters from Highfield showed little change in the usual conduct of family affairs. The children were still attending Miss Harmon's school, though they were to leave at Christmas.

Collapse of domestic order

"We are late nearly every day now you are not here to make Ernie start," wrote Mamie, almost as if it were an achievement to be proud of. "He locked the piano and threw the key in the garden, and we could none of us practice for three days. Wasn't it lovely? Letty pours out tea if mother isn't in, and yesterday she broke the teapot."

The chief items of news, however, concerned Percy. That young gentleman, with what Aunt Harriet considered his usual perversity, had sprained his ankle on the very day before he ought to have returned to school. He had been ordered to lie up on the sofa, but Winona gathered that the doctor's directions had not been very strictly carried out. She strongly suspected that the patient did not wish to recover too quickly. Whether or not that had been the case, Percy was now convalescent, and was to set off for school on the following Friday. Longworth College was not a great distance, and as Percy would have to pass through Seaton on his way, Aunt Harriet invited him to break his journey there and spend the night at her house. She had a poor opinion of the boy's capacity, but having undertaken a half share in his education she felt an increased sense of responsibility towards him, and wished to find an opportunity of a word with him in private.

Winona hailed her brother's advent with immense joy. Even so flying a visit was better than nothing. Letters were an inadequate means of expression, and she was longing to pour out all her new experiences. She wanted to tell Percy about the Symposium, and her friendship for Garnet, and the chemistry class, and the gymnasium practice, and to show him her hockey jersey which had just arrived. She had so long been the recipient of all his school news that it would be delightful to turn the tables and give him a chronicle of her own doings at the Seaton "High," which in her opinion quite rivaled

Longworth College.

To the young people's scarcely suppressed satisfaction, Miss Beach went out after tea to attend an important meeting, leaving her nephew and niece to spend the evening alone together. They had never expected such luck. As it was Friday Winona had no lessons to prepare for the next day, and could feel free for a delightful chat. She flung herself into Aunt Harriet's special big easy chair by the fireside, and lounged luxuriously, while Percy, boy-like, prowled about the room.

"Well, I'm glad you're jogging along all right," he remarked when his sister's long account came to a pause. "Though please don't for a moment compare your blessed old High School to Longworth, for they're not in the same running! Aunt Harriet hasn't quite eaten you up yet, I see?"

"She's not such a Gorgon as I expected. In fact she's been rather decent."

"The dragon's sheathed her talons? Well, that's good biz. You went off as tragic as Iphigenia, heroically declaring yourself the family sacrifice."

"Did I?" Winona had almost forgotten her original attitude of martyr. Three weeks had made a vast difference to her feelings.

"If you can peg it out in comfort with the dragon so much to the good. Shouldn't care to live here myself though. It's a dull hole. Number 10, Abbey Close wouldn't be my choice of a residence."

"Well, it's not likely you'll ever have the chance of living here!" retorted Winona, taking up the cudgels for her adopted home.

"I don't know about that," returned Percy. "The house belongs to Aunt Harriet. She'll have to leave her property to somebody, I suppose, when she shuffles off this mortal coil. I'm the eldest son, and my name's Percy Beach Woodward. That ought to count for something."

"Aunt Harriet's not going to die yet," said Winona gravely. "I think it's horrid of you to talk like this!"

"Oh, I don't wish the old girl any harm, but one may have an eye to the future all the same," was the airy response. "D'you remember Jack Cassidy who was a pupil at the Vicarage? His aunt left him five thousand pounds."

"Yes, and I heard he's muddling it away as fast as he can. Mary James told me. Her father's guardian of part of his property until he's twenty-five, you know."

"He's a topper, is Jack! He's promised to take me for a day sometime to Hartleburn, when the races are on. Now don't you go blabbing, or I'll never tell you anything again!"

"Mr. Joynson said -"

"Oh, for goodness sake shut up! A boy of sixteen isn't going to be bear-led by an old fogey like Joynson. He has the mater far too much under his finger and thumb for my taste. If you want to be chums with me, don't preach!"

Winona was silent. Her brother's infatuation for the Vicar's scapegrace ward was the affair of a year ago. She had hoped he had forgotten it. His escapades at the time, in company with his hero, had caused his mother to seek the advice and guidance of her trustee.

"Some one was telling me the other day that old oak furniture is worth a tremendous lot of money now," continued Percy, his eye roving round the room with an air almost of future proprietorship. "If that's so these things of Aunt Harriet's are a little gold mine. There was an account of a sale in the news-paper, with a picture of a cupboard that fetched two hundred pounds. It was first cousin to that!" nodding at a splendidly carved old piece which faced him.

Angela Brazil

Miss Beach's household goods were inherited from her great-grandfather, and included some fine specimens of oak, as well as rare Chippendale. Winona was too young to be a connoisseur of antiquities, but she had the curiosity to rise from her chair and join Percy in his inspection of the article in question.

"I tell you they're as alike as two peas!" he declared. "Same shape, same sort of carving, same knobs at the end! The reason why I remember the thing is that the buyer found a secret drawer in it after he'd got it home, with some old rubbish inside, and there was a lawsuit as to who owned these. He claimed he'd bought the lot with the cupboard, but the judge made him turn them up to the family of the original owner. That was why there was a picture of the cupboard in the newspaper. It put an arrow showing the place of the secret drawer. I wonder if there's one here, too? I'm going to have a try! By Jove, there is!"

A vigorous pull had dislodged a drawer in a very unexpected situation. Winona would certainly never have thought of its existence, nor would Percy, if the newspaper had not given away the secret. He looked eagerly inside.

"No treasures hidden in here! Absolutely nothing at all, except this piece of paper."

"Perhaps Aunt Harriet has never found it out," ventured Winona.

Percy did not answer immediately. He was reading the writing on the paper.

"You bet she has!" he cried at last, flushing angrily. "I never thought she'd much opinion of me, but I call this the limit! It's going where it deserves!" and acting on a sudden impulse he flung the cause of offense into the fire.

For a moment Winona did not realize what he had done. By

the time she reached the hearth the paper was already half consumed. She made a snatch at it with the tongs, but a flame sprang up and forestalled her. She had just time to read the words "last Will and Testament of me Har -" before the whole sank into ashes. She turned to her brother with a white, scared face.

"Percy! You've never burnt Aunt Harriet's will?"

Ashamed already of his impetuous act the boy nevertheless tried to bluff the matter off.

"It was an abominable shame! When I'm named Beach after her too! I wouldn't have believed it if I hadn't read it myself!" he blustered.

"Read what?"

"I shan't tell you! Look here, Win, you must promise on your honor that you'll never breathe a word about this."

"Perhaps Aunt Harriet ought to know."

"She mustn't know: *mustn't*, I tell you! I say, Win, I'm not at all sure that what I've just done isn't a chargeable offense - I believe they call it a felony. You wouldn't like to see me put into prison, would you? Then hold your tongue about it! Give me your word! Can you keep a secret?"

"I promise!" gasped Winona (Percy was squeezing her little finger nail in orthodox fashion and the agony was acute). "I promise faithfully."

She was in a terrible quandary. Her natural straightforwardness urged her to make a clean breast of the whole affair. Had she been the actual transgressor she would certainly have done so and faced the consequences. But this was Percy's secret, not her own. He was no favorite with his aunt, and so outrageous an act would prejudice him fatally in her eyes. The hint about

Angela Brazil

prison frightened Winona. She knew nothing of law, but she thought it highly probable that burning a will was a punishable crime. Suppose Aunt Harriet's rigid conscience obliged her to communicate with the police and deliver Percy into the hands of justice. Such a horrible possibility must be avoided at all costs. The sound of a latch-key in the door made her start. In a panic she rushed to the old cupboard and pushed back the secret drawer into its place. When Miss Beach entered the dining-room her nephew and niece were sitting reading by the fireside. Their choice of literature might perhaps have astonished her, for Percy was poring over Sir Oliver Lodge's "Man and the Universe," while Winona's nose was buried in Herbert Spencer's "Sociology," but if indeed she noticed it, she perhaps set it down to a laudable desire to improve their minds, and placed the matter to their credit. Percy took his departure next morning, and Winona saw him off at the railway station.

"Remember, you've to keep that business dark," he reminded her. "Aunt Harriet must never find out. She's been jawing me no end about responsibility, and looking after the kids and supporting the mater and all that. Rubbed it in hard, I can tell you! Great Juggins! Do I look like the mainstay of a family?"

As Winona watched his boyish face laughing at her from the window of the moving train she decided that he certainly did not. She sighed as she turned to leave the station. Life seemed suddenly to have assumed new perplexities. Percy's act weighed heavily on her mind. It seemed such a base return for all Aunt Harriet was doing on their behalf. She longed to thank her for her kindness and say how much she appreciated going to the High School, but she could not find the words. Theknowledge of the secret raised an extra barrier between herself and her aunt. So she sat at lunch time even shyer and more speechless than usual, and let the ball of conversation persistently drop.

"Fretting for her brother, I suppose," thought Miss Beach. "She can talk fast enough with friends of her own age. Well, I suppose an old body like myself mustn't expect to be company for a girl of fifteen!"

She was too proud to let the hurt feeling show itself on her face, however, and propping up the newspaper beside her plate, she plunged into the latest accounts from the Front.

CHAPTER VI

A CRISIS

Winona had been more than a month, nearly five weeks indeed, at the Seaton High School. In the first few days of her introduction to V.a. she had told herself that the difficulty of the work consisted largely in its newness, and that as soon as she grew accustomed to it she would sail along as swimmingly as Garnet Emerson, or Olave Parry, or Hilda Langley, or Agatha James. Most unfortunately she found her theory acted in the opposite direction. Closer acquaintance with her Form subjects proved their extreme toughness. She was not nearly up to the standard of the rest of the girls. Her Latin grammar was shaky, her French only a trifle better, she had merely a nodding acquaintance with geometry, and had not before studied chemistry. Her teacher seemed to expect her to understand many things of which she had hitherto never heard, and was apparently astounded at her ignorance. Winona puzzled over her text-books during many hours of preparation, but she made little headway. The royal road to learning, which she had fondly hoped to tread, was proving itself a stony and twisting path.

"*You* seem to get on all right?" she said wistfully to Garnet one day.

"Why, yes. Of course one has to work," admitted her friend. "Miss Huntley keeps one up to the mark. But one must expect that in V.a. They don't put scholarship holders in the Preparatory."

"I was all at sea in math. this morning."

"You were rather a duffer, certainly. The problems weren't as difficult as the ones they gave us in the entrance exam. If those didn't floor you, why couldn't you work these?"

"But they did floor me. I barely managed half the paper. I reckoned I'd failed in it."

Garnet looked surprised.

"Then your other subjects must have been extremely good to make up for it. I was told that we should probably stand or fall by maths. You were ripping in everything else, I suppose? Scored no end?"

Winona did not answer the question. She was conscious that none of her papers could have merited such an eulogium. She envied Garnet's grasp of the form work. Try as she would, her own exercises and translations were poor affairs, and her ill-trained memory found it difficult to marshal the enormous number of facts that were daily forced upon it. Miss Huntley at first was patient, but as the weeks wore on, and Winona still wallowed in a quagmire of amazing mistakes, she grew sarcastic. The girl winced under some of her cutting remarks. Apparently the mistress imagined her failure to be due to laziness and inattention, and sooner than confess that she could not understand the work, Winona was silent. She never mentioned the long hours she spent poring over her books in Aunt Harriet's dining-room. After all, it was better to be thought idle than stupid. But it was humiliating to feel that she was counted among the slackers of the Form, while Garnet was already winning laurels. The contrast between the two scholarship holders could not fail to be noticed.

Miss Huntley (privately known to the Form as "Bunty") was a clever, but rather remorseless teacher. She had been on the staff since the opening of the school two years before, and she was determined at all costs to maintain the high standard inaugurated at its foundation. She was herself the product of High School education, and knew to the last scruple how much to require from girls in V.a. To those who appeared to be really trying their best she was ready to give intelligent help, but she had no mercy for slackers. She was possessed of a certain amount of dry humor, greatly appreciated by the form *en bloc*, though each quaked privately lest, through some unlucky slip, she might find herself the object of the smart but withering satires. Despite her strictness, "Bunty" was popular. She was an admirable tennis player, and a formidable champion in a match "Mistresses *v.* Girls." Her strong personality fascinated Winona, who would have done much to gain her approval. So far, however, she was entirely on Miss Huntley's black list.

Matters came to a crisis over a difficult bit of Vergil. Latin was, next to mathematics, the most painfully wobbling of Winona's shaky subjects. She had puzzled in vain over this particular piece of translation. The words, indeed, she had found in the dictionary, but she could not twist them into sense.

"Old Vergil's utterly stumped me to-day!" she mourned to Garnet, as they met in the dressing-room before nine o'clock. "If Bunty puts me to construe anywhere on page 21, I'm a gone coon. I'm feeling in a blue funk, I can tell you."

"Poor old bluebottle! Don't wrinkle up your forehead like that - you're making permanent lines! It's a bad trick, and just spoils you."

"I can't help it when I'm worried!"

"Then don't worry."

"Oh, it's easy enough for you; you don't have to receive the vials of Bunty's scorn."

Winona hoped against hope that the difficult page might fall to somebody else's turn. Miss Huntley took no particular order, but selected girls at random to construe the lesson. In a Form of twenty it was possible not to be chosen at all. Winona kept very quiet, so as not to attract the mistress' attention. Marjorie Kemp and Olave Parry had already translated half of the fatal page, with tolerable credit. Miss Huntley's eye was wandering in the direction of Irene Mills. Winona dared to breathe. Then, alas! alas! Some unlucky star caused the mistress to look back towards the middle of the room. In a spasm of nervousness, Winona jerked her elbow, and away went her pencil-box, clattering on to the floor, and dispersing its collection of pens, pencils, nibs and other treasures beneath the neighboring desks. There was a dead silence, and the culprit was instantly the center of attention.

"A clumsy thing to do! Leave those things where they are! You can pick them up after the lesson," observed Miss Huntley grimly. "Go on now with the translation."

Winona's hot face had been hidden under Audrey Redfern's desk. She rose reluctantly. Her confusion made the hard passage seem twice as difficult. Even the words which she had carefully looked up in the dictionary and learned by heart escaped her fickle memory. She stumbled and floundered hopelessly, getting redder and redder with shame. Miss Huntley preserved an ominous silence, and did not attempt to help her out.

"That will do!" she said, at the end of about eight lines. "After such a complete exhibition of incompetence we won't inflict any more of your bungling upon the form. We must see if we can find a way of sharpening your wits. Your brain seems to have been lying fallow since you came to school! You will report yourself to Miss Bishop at four o'clock this afternoon."

The rest of the morning passed like a bad dream to Winona. It was a rare event for a teacher to send a girl to the head mistress. The prospect of the coming interview made her cold with apprehension. She avoided Garnet at one o'clock, and hurried out of the dressing-room without speaking to any one.

She had a wild project of pleading a headache, and begging Aunt Harriet to let her stop at home for the rest of the day. But then to-morrow's explanations would be infinitely worse. No, it was better to face the horrible ordeal and get it over. As it happened, Miss Beach had gone out to lunch, so that leave of absence was an impossibility. Winona ate her early dinner alone.

"Aren't you well, miss? Would you like me to make you a cup of tea?" asked Alice the housemaid, noticing that the pudding was unappreciated, and divining that something must be amiss.

"No, thanks! I'm in a hurry, and must fly off to school as quickly as I can. It's my early afternoon."

Winona had a music lesson at a quarter past two on Thursdays. It was always rather a rush to get back in time for it. She crammed her "Bach's Preludes" and "Schubert's Impromptus" automatically into her portfolio, and started. It was only when she was half-way down Church Street that she remembered she had left her book of studies on the top of the piano. Needless to say, her lesson that day was hardly a success. In the disturbed state of her mind she was quite incapable of concentrating her attention on music. Miss Catteral looked surprised at her wrong notes and imperfect phrasing.

"I shall expect to find some improvement in this 'Impromptu' next week," she remarked. "Have you practiced your hour daily? You must take these bars, which I have marked, separately, and play each twenty times in succession, slowly at first and then faster, and remember here that it is the left hand which gives the melody, and the right is only the accompaniment. I thought you had sufficient music in you to appreciate that! The way you thumped out those chords was painful. I am not pleased at all."

Miss Catteral so rarely scolded that Winona felt doubly humiliated. It was all a part and parcel of the general ill-luck of the day. She fetched her drawing-board, and went to the art class. Here at least she would have peace for an hour, though every one of the sixty minutes was bringing her nearer to her dreaded interview. At four o'clock, with a horrible sinking feeling in her heart, and a trembling sensation in her knees, she knocked at the door of the head-mistress's study, and entered in response to the "Come in!" which followed. Miss Bishop looked up from some papers, motioned her to a chair, and went on writing for several minutes. To Winona it seemed worse than waiting at the dentist's. The suspense was ghastly.

At last the Principal paused, laid down her pen, and blotted her pages.

"Come here, Winona Woodward," she said quietly. "I wish to have a straight talk with you."

Miss Bishop's eyes were her most striking feature. They were large and clear, but the pupils were unusually small, appearing mere black specks in the midst of a wide circle of blue. This peculiarity gave her a particularly intense and penetrating expression. Winona, standing at attention beside the desk, dropped her own eyes before the steady, searching gaze.

"Miss Huntley's report of your work is not at all satisfactory," began Miss Bishop. "I have been watching your progress since you joined the school, and I cannot think you are trying your best. At first, when you were totally new to your Form, I suspended judgment, but you have been here nearly half a term now - quite long enough to accustom yourself to our methods. I confess I am greatly disappointed. I had hoped for better things from the holder of a County Scholarship."

Winona remained silent. She could think of nothing to say in self-defense.

"It must be sheer lack of grit and effort," continued Miss Bishop. "I cannot understand how a girl who did so remarkably well in the entrance examination can rest content with such a low record. How long do you take over your preparation?"

"Until my aunt sends me to bed," replied Winona, in a very subdued voice. "I spend the whole evening at my lessons."

Miss Bishop looked puzzled.

"Then the work must be too difficult for you. If that is the case, I must remove you to V.b."

V.b. was notorious in the school as a refuge for incompetence. It was mainly composed of girls of sixteen and seventeen who could not reach the standard of the Sixth, and who went by the nickname of "owls" or "stupids." The prospect of being relegated to such an intellectual backwater spread palpable dismay over Winona's face. Miss Bishop smiled rather grimly.

"We can't win honors without paying the price! You must know that already by experience. I conclude that you studied hard for the Scholarship examination? Well, your Form work requires equally close application. Here is Miss Huntley's report: 'French, weak; Latin, beneath criticism; mathematics, extremely bad.' Yet in all these three subjects you gained a high percentage in the entrance examination. I have your papers here - yes, Latin 85, French 87, mathematics 92" (rapidly turning over the pages), "it is simply incredible how you have fallen off."

Winona was gazing at the sheets of foolscap in the Principal's hand.

"Those aren't my papers," she faltered.

"Certainly they are. They're marked with your number, 11."

"But I wasn't number 11, I was number 10."

Miss Bishop stooped, opened a drawer in her bureau, and took out a book.

"Here it is in black and white," she replied. "No. 11, Winona Woodward."

Winona's shaking hands clutched the edge of the bureau. In a flash the whole horrible truth was suddenly revealed to her. Until that moment she had almost forgotten how she and the ruddy-haired girl had collided at the door of the examination-room, and dropped their cards. In picking them up, they must have effected an exchange. She remembered that she had been too agitated to notice her number until after the accident had happened. She now related the circumstance as best she could. Miss Bishop listened aghast.

"What number did you say you took in the examination-room? Ten? That is entered in my book as Marjorie Kaye. I have the rest of the candidates' papers in this bundle. Let me see - yes, here is No. 10. Is this your handwriting? Then I'm afraid there has been a terrible blunder, and the scholarship has been awarded to the wrong girl."

The Principal's consternation was equalled by Winona's. To the latter the ground seemed slipping from under her feet. She tried to speak, but failed. A great lump rose in her throat. For a moment the room whirled round.

"This set of papers, No. 10, was marked so low as to be out of the running," continued Miss Bishop. "It is a most unfortunate mistake, and places the school in an extremely awkward position. I must consult with the Governors at once. Pending their decision, it will be better not to mention the matter to anybody. You may go now."

Winona managed somehow to get herself out of the study, to put on her hat and coat, and to walk home to Abbey Close. Her aunt was still absent, for which she was intensely thankful, and ignoring the tea that was waiting on the dining-room table, she rushed upstairs to her bedroom. Her one imperative need was to be alone. She must face the situation squarely. Her world had suddenly turned topsy-turvy; instead of being the winner of the County Scholarship, she was among the rejected candidates. In her heart of hearts she had always marveled how her indifferent papers could have scored such a success. She wondered this explanation had never occurred to her before. All this time she had been wearing another girl's laurels. What was going to happen next? She supposed the scholarship would be taken from her, and given to its rightful owner. And herself? She would probably be packed home, as Percy had prophesied, "like a whipped puppy." Possibly Aunt Harriet might offer to pay her fee as an ordinary pupil at the High School, but in either case the humiliation would be supreme.

Winona dreaded returning home. In spite of the difficulty of the work, the High School had opened a fresh world to her. She could never again be content with the old rut. Miss Harmon's dull lessons would be intolerable, and life without Garnet's friendship would seem a blank. The companionship of her three little sisters was totally inadequate for a girl who was fast growing up. She shrank from speculating how her mother would receive the bad news. Mrs. Woodward was one of those parents who expect their children to gain the prizes which they were incapable of winning for themselves. She had claimed a kind of second-hand credit in her daughter's triumph. Winona knew from past experience that so keen a disappointment would involve a string of reproaches, regrets and fretting. She would probably never hear the last of it. The family hopes had been pinned upon her success, and to frustrate them was to court utter disgrace. For the present she must live with this sword of Damocles hanging over her head, but she hoped the Governors would decide the matter speedily, and put her out of her misery.

There is one virtue in a supreme trouble - it dwarfs all minor griefs. Percy's secret, which had been felt as a continual burden, seemed to sink into comparative obscurity, and the worry of school work and the dread of Miss Huntley's sarcasm were mere flies in the ointment. Winona never quite knew how she got through the week that followed. It stayed afterwards in her memory as a period of black darkness, a valley of humiliation, in which her old childish self slipped away, and a new, stronger and more capable personality was born to face the future. She had resigned herself so utterly to the inevitable, that when at last Miss Bishop's summons came, she was able to walk quite calmly into the study. The Principal was seated as usual at her bureau; Winona's entrance examination papers lay before her. Her manner was non-committal; her blue eyes looked even more penetrating than usual.

"You will have been wondering what was going to happen about the matter of the scholarship," she began.

"Yes, Miss Bishop," answered Winona meekly. She did not add that she had spent eight days in a mental purgatory.

"I of course placed the facts before the Governors, and we at once communicated with the parents of Marjorie Kaye. We find, however, that in the meantime she has been elected a scholar of the Maria Harvey Foundation, and will therefore be unable to accept this scholarship. Her papers and those of Garnet Emerson were the only ones of outstanding merit. In re-examining the remaining eighteen we find a uniform level of mediocrity. As regards your set of papers, the general standard is low, with one exception. We consider that your essay on Lady Jane Grey shows an originality and a capacity for thought which may be worthy of training. On the strength of this - and this alone - the Governors have decided to allow you to retain your scholarship. In so doing they are perfectly within their rights. They did not undertake to grant free tuition to the candidate who scored the highest number of marks, but to the one who, in their opinion, was most likely to benefit by the school course. It was a matter to be settled entirely at their discretion. I have carefully re-read your papers, and compared them with your form record, and I come to the conclusion that you are backward and ill-instructed in many subjects, but that you are not idle or stupid. I shall make arrangements for you to have special coaching in mathematics, Latin and chemistry until you can keep up with the rest of the Form. I find your reports for history and English literature are good, which confirms my opinion that you do not lack ability. You will need to work very hard, especially at those subjects in which you are so deficient, but I trust you will soon show a marked improvement, and thus justify the decision of the Governors. Are you prepared to try?"

"I don't know how to thank you - I'll do my very best!" stammered Winona, quite overcome by this unexpected *denouement*.

"Then that is all that need be said. Miss Lever will take you every day from 3.30 to 4.15 for private tuition. Mark that on your time-table, and go to her this afternoon in the Preparatory Room. You may tell Miss Garside that I am disengaged now, and at liberty to speak to her."

Winona left the study with very different feelings from those with which she had entered. Her spirits were so high that she wanted to dance along the corridor. She could hardly believe her good fortune. Those great and important gentlemen, the Governors, had actually approved of her essay to the extent of allowing it to stand as her qualification for the Scholarship! She blessed Lady Jane Grey, and Edgar Allan Poe, and Browning, and Andre de Chenier, and the happy chance that had made her combine them all. She was glad she had paid that visit to Hampton Court, and that she had seen Lady Jane Grey's portrait, and had been able to describe both. Life was going to be a very exhilarating business, now her position in the school was once more secure.

"I'll show them how I can work," she thought. "They shan't be sorry that they let me stay after all! Oh, I am in luck! Yes, I'm the luckiest girl in the school!"

CHAPTER VII

AN AUTUMN FORAY

Winona felt that she now started life at the High School on an entirely new basis. Miss Bishop and Miss Huntley understood her limitations and judged her accordingly. It was not by any means that they lowered their standard, but that they appreciated her difficulty in keeping up with the Form and gave her credit for her hard work. And hard work it undoubtedly was. She would get up early in the morning to revise her lessons before breakfast, and would sit toiling over books and exercises in the evenings till even Aunt Harriet - indefatigable worker herself - would tell her to stop, and wax moral on the folly of burning the candle at both ends. The coaching from Miss Lever was of inestimable value. It supplied just the gaps in which she was deficient, and gave her an adequate grasp of her three toughest subjects. Slowly she began to make headway, she saw light in mathematical problems that had before been meaningless formulae, chemistry was less of a hopeless tangle, and Vergil's lines construed into understandable sentences instead of utter nonsense. It was only gradual progress, however. She had much ground to cover before she caught up the Form. She was plodding, but not a brilliant all-round scholar like Garnet. The fact was that Winona was only clever in one direction: in the realm of imagination her mind ran like a racehorse, but harnessed to heavy intellectual burdens it proved but a sorry steed.

It was fortunate for both her health and her spirits that head

Angela Brazil

work did not represent the only side of school activities. Miss Bishop was wise enough to lay much stress on physical development. A ten minutes' drill was part of the daily routine, a gymnasium practice was held twice a week, and Wednesday afternoons were devoted to hockey. In addition to this the girls played tennis on the asphalt courts during the winter and spring terms, whenever the weather was suitable, and basket ball was constantly going on in the playground. Athletics was decidedly the fashionable cult of the school. Kirsty Paterson, as Games Captain, made it her business to see that nobody slacked without justifiable cause. She would break up knots of chatting idlers, and cajole them forth to "cultivate muscle" as she expressed it, while her keen eye was quick to note anybody's "points" and employ them for the general benefit. Kirsty's jolly, breezy manner and strict sense of justice made her an admirable captain. She was highly popular with juniors as well as seniors, for she took the trouble to organize the games of the little girls as carefully as those of their elders.

"It's insane short-sighted policy to neglect the kids," was her creed. "Now's the time to be training them. Get them thoroughly well in hand and make them understand what's expected from them, and in four or five years' time they'll be crack players. Yes, I know it's looking far ahead, and we prefects won't be here to see the result, but the school will reap the benefit some day and that's the main thing to aim at. I'm proud of my cadets and, in the future, when they're winning laurels for the Seaton High, perhaps they'll remember I started them on the right track. 'Keep up the standard all round' is going to be the motto while I'm Captain."

To Winona athletics and organized games came as a revelation. She had a slim wiry little figure and was a good runner, with a capacity for keeping her breath, and had also a considerable power of spring, all of which stood her in good stead both in the hockey field and in the gymnasium. Though Kirsty said little, she could feel her efforts were being watched and approved, and the knowledge gave her a tingling sense of satisfaction. It was delightful to feel that she was a factor in this big school, and that she was doing her bit - however insignificant - to help up the athletic standard. In physical agility Winona was superior to Garnet. She could beat her easily at tennis, and there was already a wide gap between their gymnastic achievements. It was a fortunate circumstance, for it just balanced their friendship, and put them on a footing of equality which would have been otherwise absent. Garnet, so manifestly first in Form work, possessed of greater confidence and *savoir faire* in school life and older in experience for her years than Winona, might have monopolized the lead too entirely, had she not been obliged to yield the palm of outdoor sports to her friend.

Garnet was, in truth, just a trifle inclined to "boss." She liked Winona, and wanted her for a chum, but she loved to lay down the law and to constitute herself an authority upon every possible subject. There was no doubt it was owing to her initiative that the two scholarship-holders were gaining a position for themselves in the school. As Garnet had foreseen, the part they had taken in the Symposium won them favorable recognition. To be singled out as soloists and to have the honor of playing an accompaniment for the prefects had raised them above the common herd, and though a few were jealous, more were ready to extend the hand of good fellowship. In their own Form they were living down the prejudice which had at first existed against them. Hilda Langley and Estelle Harrison were not very friendly and influenced Olave Parry and Mollie Hill against them, but these formed a minority, and the bulk of the girls seemed to have decided in their favor.

With the enormous demands made on her time by her home preparation, Winona did not venture to join many of the school guilds. She would have liked immensely to put her name down for election to the Dramatic Society, the Debating Club and the Literary Association, but these all required rather strenuous brain work from their members, and in the circumstances she knew it would be folly to take them up. At some future date, when her ordinary subjects proved less of a burden, she promised herself the pleasure of being numbered among that select clique known as "The Intellectuals," but for the present her motto must be "grim grind." The Patriotic Knitting Guild seemed more feasible. She paid her subscription, received her skeins of khaki wool, and started mittens to fill up odd moments. She found the knitting a soothing occupation, it could be taken up and laid down so easily; it often went to school with her, and would come out during the interval, or while she was waiting for a class. The Photographic Union was beyond her, for as yet she had no camera, but she thought she was justified in joining the Natural History League. This society did not for the present demand papers from its members, but contented itself with encouraging the collection of objects for the school museum. Its main activities would be during the summer term, though a weather record was kept throughout the year, and any nature notes that were worthy of being written down were duly chronicled in the Field Book. Linda Fletcher and Annie Hardy, two of the prefects, were the leading spirits in the League. Linda was great on entomology, and, having a brother who was interested in the subject, had been out "sugaring" in his company in August and September, and had secured some fine specimens of moths. She had boxes full of chrysalides which she fondly hoped would emerge in the spring into perfect insects, and she had made quite a good little collection of beetles. Annie was more interested in botany, she pressed flowers and leaves, dried fruits and seed vessels, and made praiseworthy efforts at preserving funguses in bottles, though these latter attempts were not always attended with the success they deserved, as they were apt to acquire a gamey odor, to which her mother very naturally objected, and she would be obliged disconsolately to turn them out into the dust-bin.

November happened to be a particularly fine month at Seaton. There had been little rain, and no high winds to blow the leaves away. Though the trees in the city were bare, those in the country round about remained almost in their October glory, and in sheltered woods some were still green. The persistent sunshine encouraged the Natural History League to plan an excursion for its members, and after a consultation with Miss Lever, the Botany mistress, Linda pinned up the following announcement on the school notice board: -

NATURAL HISTORY LEAGUE.

An Autumn Foray will be held on Saturday next, visiting Monkend Woods and Copplestone Quarry. Members will meet at station for the 12.45 train to Powerscroft, returning by the 5.30 from Chartwell. Tea at farm-house. Walking distance five miles. Leaders: Miss Lever, Linda Fletcher and Annie Hardy. Those intending to join kindly give their names to the Secretary on Wednesday at latest.

L. FLETCHER,

Hon. Sec.

The prospect of a ramble was alluring. Winona was a country lover, so she forthwith secured Aunt Harriet's permission for the outing and placed her name upon the list.

"I don't think there'll be more than a dozen of us altogether," said Linda, "but really a small party's more manageable than a big one, and I'll undertake we enjoy ourselves. Miss Lever can get permission for us to walk through the private part of the woods - there's no shooting this autumn, you know - so that will be simply glorious, and she says we ought to find some fossils in the quarry, if we've luck. I hope the weather will keep up. Don't forget to take a vasculum or a basket, and a hammer for fossils, and be sure you put on strong boots. The tea will probably be eightpence a head. Miss Lever is writing before-hand to the farm to make arrangements."

Garnet also was to join the excursion and she promised to call for Winona, so that they might walk to the station together. The latter had an early lunch, and was ready dressed and waiting for her friend by twenty minutes past twelve. Garnet's tram was late, and by the time she reached Abbey Close the clock pointed to the half-hour.

"I'm frightfully sorry! You must think me a Juggins, but it wasn't my fault!" she apologized. "We shall have to sprint, but we'll just do it."

The girls set off at a tremendous pace along the Close and down the Abbey avenue, but it was difficult to keep the same speed through the town, where the streets were thronged with country people who had come in for the Saturday market. They got along as best they could, walking first on the pavement and then on the road, dodging round stout females bearing baskets, avoiding hooting motors, and finally making a dash down a back street that led to the railway bridge. They clattered down the steps to the booking office, secured their tickets and rushed on to the platform. The hands of the big clock were at 12.45 exactly, the guard was about to wave his green flag. They were too late to look for their party; they simply pelted towards the nearest carriage, a porter opened the door and they scrambled in just in the very nick of time.

"Oh, thank goodness! Thank goodness!" gasped Garnet. "I thought we'd miss it! I never had such a run in my life before! Oh! It's given me a stitch in my side!"

"They've put us in a first!" exulted Winona, breathlessly. "We have it all to ourselves! What luck! Hope they won't make a fuss about our tickets when we get out!"

"It was the porter's fault. He opened the door. We'll ask Miss Lever to explain. I suppose the others are further along some-where in the train. I wonder if they saw us get in?"

"If they didn't, it will be a surprise packet for them when we turn up."

"Yes, they'll have made up their minds we're left behind."

The two girls leaned back, enjoying the luxury of traveling in a first-class compartment. They felt the excursion had begun well as far as they were concerned. Their satisfaction was short-lived, however. When they neared Barnhill, the train, instead of stopping, rushed through the station at thirty-five miles an hour. Garnet turned to Winona in utter consternation.

"Oh, good-night!" she ejaculated. "I verily believe we've gone and got into the express!"

They saw at once how it had happened. The 12.40 fast train to Rockfield must have been five minutes late. In their hurry they had mistaken it for the stopping train, which probably had been drawn up behind it in the station.

"Well, this is a pretty go!" agreed Winona. "We shall be carried on to Rockfield and have to come back."

"We shall miss the ramble! Oh, it's the limit of hard luck - to see ourselves whizzing through Powerscroft!"

"I say, I believe we're stopping after all!"

They let down the window and looked out. They were still about a mile from Powerscroft, but the train drew up, probably in obedience to an adverse signal. Then the girls did a terrible and awful thing. They never remembered afterwards which suggested it, probably the idea occurred to both simultaneously, but in defiance of the law of the realm and the rules of the railway company, they opened the door of the carriage and climbed down on to the line. There were some railings near, and they scrambled over these and dodged down an embankment into a coppice before anybody in the train had time to give an alarm. They hoped their flight had not been noticed, but of that they could not be sure. They hid behind some bushes until they heard the train rumble away.

"That was the smartest thing we've ever done in our lives!" chuckled Garnet. "I believe we could be fined about ten pounds each if they caught us!"

Angela Brazil

"Let us hurry on and try to find the road," said Winona, who was rather frightened at her own temerity, and had a nervous apprehension lest a guard or a signalman or some other railway official might even now be in pursuit and arrest them on a charge of breaking the law.

After crossing a field they struck a path which led them eventually into a by-lane.

"I know where we are," affirmed Garnet. "I bicycled this way once. Monkend Woods are in that direction, and if we turn to the left and through this village we shall get there sooner than the others, I believe, and be waiting for them when they arrive. Their train won't have reached Powerscroft yet."

"We'd better step out all the same," urged Winona.

Fortunately Garnet possessed the bump of locality. Her recollection of the district was correct, and after a brisk walk of about a mile they found themselves in the high road close to the wood, and sat down on a wall to wait. Their fast train and short cut had given them an advantage: it was nearly half an hour before they spied the rest of the party strolling leisurely up the hill with baskets and vasculums. The surprise of the League at seeing them was immense, and naturally there were many inquiries as to how they had thus stolen a march upon their friends.

"Oh, we came in an aeroplane!" said Garnet jauntily. "It just dropped us in the field over there. Very pleasant run, though a little chilly in the clouds!"

She was obliged to own up, however, in answer to Miss Lever's inquiries, give a precise account of their adventure, and cry "peccavi."

"Of course Dollikins had to be orthodox and preach a short sermon," she confided afterwards to Winona, "but I'm sure she'd have done the same thing herself in the circumstances. I could see admiration in her eye, although she talked about running risks and the possibility of broken necks."

Miss Lever, otherwise Dollikins, from the fact that her Christian name was Dorothy, held high favor among the girls. She was brisk and jolly, decidedly athletic, and a first-rate leader of outdoor expeditions. She had called at the gamekeeper's cottage *en route* and shown the letter of permission from the owner of the property, so that the party was able to explore the wood with a clear conscience, despite the trespass notice nailed on to the gate. And what a delightful wood it was! To enter it was like stepping into one of Grimm's fairy tales. An avenue of splendid pines reared their dark boughs against a russet background of beeches; everywhere the leaves seemed to have donned their brightest and gayest tints, as if bidding a last good-by before they fell from the trees. The undergrowth was gorgeous: bramble, elder, honeysuckle, briony, rowan, and alder vied with one another in the vividness of their crimson and orange, while the bracken was a sea of pale gold. There were all sorts of delightful things to be found - acorns lay so plentifully in the pathway that the girls could not help scrunching them underfoot. A few were already sending out tiny shoots in anticipation of spring, and these were carefully saved to take home and grow in bottles. A stream ran through the wood, its banks almost completely covered with vivid green mosses, in sheets so thick and compact that a slight pull would raise a yard at a time. Some resembled tufted tassels, some the most delicate ferns, and others showed the split cups of their seed-vessels like pixie goblets. Annie Hardy, whose experienced eyes were on the look-out for certain botanical treasures reported to grow at Monkend, was searching among the dead twigs under the hazel bushes, and was rewarded by finding a clump of the curious little birds-nest fungus with its seeds packed like tiny eggs inside. Some orange elf-cups, a bright red toadstool or two, and a few of the larger purple varieties that had lingered on from October made quite a creditable fungus record for the League, and specimens of wild flowers were also secured, a belated foxglove or two, a clump of ragwort, some blue harebells, campion, herb-robert, buttercup, yarrow, thistle, and actually a strawberry blossom. The leaders had brought note-books and wrote down each find as reported by the members, taking the specimens for Miss Lever to verify if there were any doubt as to identification. Animal and bird life was not absent. Shy bunnies whisked away, showing a dab of white tail as they dived under the bracken; a splendid squirrel ran across the path and darted up an oak tree, a wood-pigeon whirred from a pine top, a great woodpecker, scared by their approach, started from the bushes and flew past them so near that they could see the green flash of its wings and the red markings on its head, while a whole fluttering flight of long-tailed tits were flitting like a troop of fairies round the hole of a lichen-covered beech.

Miss Lever was as enthusiastic as the girls; she climbed over fallen tree trunks, grubbed among dead leaves, jumped the brook and scaled fences with delightful energy. It was she who pointed out the heron sailing overhead, and noticed the gold-crested wren's nest hanging under the branch of a fir, a little battered with autumn rain, and too high, alas! to be taken, but a most interesting item to go down in the note-books. The girls could hardly be persuaded to tear themselves away from the glory of the woods, and would have spent the whole time there, but Miss Lever had other plans.

"Come along! We've scared the pheasants quite enough," she declared. "My mind is set on fossils, and if we don't go on to Copplestones at once we shall be caught in the dark, or miss our tea or our train or something equally disagreeable."

The quarry was only half a mile away, and it proved as interesting as the wood. Being Saturday afternoon the men were not working, so they had the place to themselves, and wandered about examining heaps of shale, and tapping likely-looking stones with their hammers. Garnet and Winona knew nothing of geology, so they listened with due meekness while the instructed few discoursed learnedly on palaeozoic rocks, stratified conglomerates and quartzites. They rejoiced with Miss Lever, however, when she secured a fairly intact belemnite. It was the only good find they had, though some of the girls got broken bits of fossil shells.

"The fact is one needs a whole day to hunt about in this quarry, and my watch tells me we ought to be going," said Miss Lever. "Who feels inclined for tea?"

Everybody felt very much disposed, so the procession started off cheerfully for the farm close by, and the nature-lovers were soon hard at work consuming platefuls of bread and butter, jars of jam, and piles of plum cake.

"Sixteen varieties of wild flowers, seven various specimens of fungi, nine different sorts of berries, twelve species of birds noticed, also rabbits and squirrel, one bird's nest and one perfect fossil - not a bad record for an autumn foray!" said Linda, proudly consulting her note-book.

"Especially when you remember we're well on in November!" added Annie. "It will be something to enter in the League minutes book."

"I'm afraid it's the last ramble we shall get this year," said Miss Lever, "but I've one or two nice little schemes on hand for the spring, so the League must look forward to next April. Will any one have any more tea? Then please make a move, for it's time we were starting."

"Good old Dollikins!" murmured Linda as the girls put on their coats. "She's A1 at a foray. Got something ripping for next season in her head. I can tell by the twinkle in her eye. She'll ruminate over it all winter, and drop it on us as a surprise some day. Oh, thunder! Yes, we ought to be starting! Come along, you slackers, do you want to be left standing on the platform with a couple of hours to wait for the next train? Then sprint as hard as you can!"

Angela Brazil

CHAPTER VIII

CONCERNS A CAMERA

Winona went home at Christmas with a whole world of new experiences to call her own. Her first term had indeed been an epoch in her life, and though the holidays were naturally welcome, she felt that she could look forward with pleasure to the next session of school. Her family received her with a certain amount of respect. The younger ones listened enviously to her accounts of hockey matches and symposiums, and began to wish Fate had wafted their fortunes to Seaton. They had left Miss Harmon's little school, and next term were expecting, with some apprehension, a governess whom Aunt Harriet had recommended. Winona, who after thirteen weeks at Abbey Close found the home arrangements rather chaotic, could not help privately endorsing Miss Beach's wisdom in instituting such a change. Poor Mrs. Woodward had been greatly out of health for the last few months, and kept much to her bedroom, while the children had been running wild in a quite deplorable fashion. Letty, who ought to have had some influence over the others, was the naughtiest of all, and the ringleader in every mischievous undertaking. Having occupied the position of "eldest" for thirteen weeks, she was not at all disposed to submit to her sister's authority, and there were many tussles between the two.

"You'll *have* to do as your governess tells you, when she comes!" protested Winona on one particularly urgent occasion.

"All right, Grannie!" retorted Letty pertly. "I'll settle that matter with the good lady herself, and in the meantime I'm not going to knuckle under to you, so don't think it! You needn't come back so precious high and mighty from your High School, and expect to boss the whole show here. So there!"

And Winona, who aforetime had been able to subdue her unruly sister, found herself baffled, for their mother was ill, and must not be disturbed, and Percy, who might have been on her side, would only lie on the sofa and guffaw.

"Fight it out, like a pair of Kilkenny cats!" was his advice. "I'll sweep up the fragments that remain of you afterwards. No, I'm not going to back either of you. Go ahead and get it over!"

Percy had grown immensely during this last term. He was now seventeen, and very tall, though at present decidedly lanky. The Cadet Corps at his school absorbed most of his interests. He held emphatic opinions upon the war, and aired them daily to his family over the morning paper. According to his accounts, matters seemed likely to make little progress until he and his contemporaries at Longworth College should have reached military age, and be able to take their due part in the struggle, at which happy crisis the Germans would receive a setback that would astonish the Kaiser.

"Our British tactics have been all wrong!" he declared. "I can tell you we follow things out inch by inch at Longworth, and you should just hear what Johnstone Major has to say. Some of those generals at the Front are old women! They ought to send them home, and set them some knitting to do. If I'd the ordering of affairs I'd give the command to fellows under twenty-five! New wine should be in new bottles."

The younger children listened with admiration to Percy's views on war topics, much regretting that the Government had not yet obtained the benefit of his advice. Godfrey even hoped that the war would not be over before there was a chance for precept to be put into practice, and already, in imagination, saw his brother in the uniform of a Field Marshal. Winona smiled tolerantly. She took Percy's opinions for what they were worth. If his school report was anything to go by, he had certainly not won laurels at Longworth this term, in the direction of brainwork, and the headmaster's comment: "Lacking in steady application," had probably been amply justified.

Winona was not altogether happy about Percy, these holidays. Jack Cassidy was spending Christmas at the Vicarage, and claimed much of his time, and the influence was not altogether for good. Young Cassidy had already given the Vicar, his guardian and former tutor, considerable trouble. At twenty-two he had run through a large proportion of the money which had come to him at his majority, though fortunately he could not touch the bulk of his property till he should be twenty-five. At present he was waiting for a commission, and amusing himself as best he could in the village until the welcome missive should arrive. For lack of other congenial companions he sought Percy's society. Neither Mr. James, the Vicar, nor Mrs. Woodward realized how much the two young fellows were together, or they certainly would not have encouraged the intimacy. Winona, who was just old enough to recognize certain undesirable features, tackled Percy in private.

"Mother wouldn't like your going into 'The Blue Harp,' and playing billiards with Jack!" she remonstrated. "You were there hours yesterday. Doesn't it cost a lot?"

"Oh, Jack pays for it! At least he settles with old Chubbs. I have a bit on the score, of course, but he says that can wait a while. I'm improving, and I'll beat him yet, and win my own back."

"You promised mother you wouldn't bet again, after what happened last Easter."

"Now don't you go jaw-wagging!"

"Well, I must say something! If Mr. Joynson -"

"Old Joynson may go and boil his head! I'm seventeen now. Look here, Win, if you're going to turn sneak -"

"Sneak, indeed! Do I ever tell your secrets? Think what you did at Aunt Harriet's!"

Percy changed color.

"You've not breathed a word about that?"

"Of course I haven't, but I'm always terrified that she'll find out."

"It was a rocky little business. I say, Win, I was looking up wills in 'Every Man his Own Lawyer.' If Aunt Harriet died intestate all her estate would go to her next-of-kin, and that's Uncle Herbert Beach out in China. The mater wouldn't have a look-in, because her mother was only Aunt Harriet's half-sister. Uncle Herbert would just get the lot. She ought to make another will at once."

"Had you better tell, then?" faltered Winona.

"Tell? Certainly not! But you might very well suggest it to her. You've plenty of opportunities, as you're living there. Bring the conversation round to wills, and ask casually if she's made hers."

"Oh, I couldn't!"

"Yes, you could. You ought to do it, Winona. The mater stands to lose everything as it is. It would probably make Aunt Harriet look inside the drawer, and then she'd see her paper was gone."

"And suspect us!"

"Why should she know we'd had anything to do with it? The servants might have been rummaging. I certainly think it's your duty, Win, to take some steps."

It was rather fine to hear Percy preaching duty on a subject in which he was so plainly a defaulter. Winona at first indignantly repudiated the task he wished to impose upon her. Nevertheless, the idea kept returning and troubling her. She was sure Aunt Harriet ought to know that the will had been destroyed, and if it was impossible to tell her outright, this would certainly be a means of putting her on the track. Winona's whole soul revolted from the notion of speculating upon possible advantages to be gained from a relative's death. She would rather let Uncle Herbert inherit everything than interfere for herself. But for her mother it was a different matter. Aunt Harriet might wish her goddaughter to receive part of her fortune, and to conceal the destruction of the will might mean depriving Mrs. Woodward of a handsome legacy. How to make Miss Beach realize the loss of the paper without getting Percy into trouble was a problem that might have perplexed older and wiser heads.

Meanwhile it was holiday time, and there were many more pleasant subjects to think about. Winona's Christmas present had been a small hand camera, the very thing for which she had longed during the whole of the past term. She contemplated it with the utmost satisfaction. Now she would be able to join the Photographic Club at school, to go out on some of the Saturday afternoon expeditions, and to have a few of her prints in the Exhibition. She could take snap-shots of the girls and the classroom, and make them into picture postcards to send to her mother, and she could make a series of home photos to hang up in her bedroom at Abbey Close. There seemed no limit indeed to the possibilities of her new camera. She guarded it jealously from the prying fingers of the younger members of the family.

"Paws off!" she commanded. "Anybody who interferes with this Kodak will quarrel with me, so I give you full and fair warning! Oh, yes, Dorrie! I dare say you'd just like to press the button! I'd guarantee your fairy fingers to smash anything! It's 'mustn't touch, only look' where this is concerned. No personal familiarities, please!"

December and January were scarcely propitious months for the taking of snap-shots, but Winona attempted some time exposures, with varying results. It was difficult to make the children realize the necessity of keeping absolutely still, and they spoilt several of her plates by grinning or moving. She secured quite a nice photo of the house, however, and several of the village, and promised herself better luck with family portraits when the summer came round again. She turned a large cupboard in the attic into her dark-room, and spent many hours dabbling among chemicals. She had urgent offers of help, but rejected them steadfastly, greatly to the disapp-ointment of her would-be assistants. Her sanctum became a veritable Bluebeard's chamber, for to prevent possible accidents she locked the door, and kept the key perpetually in her pocket during the day time, sleeping with it under her pillow at night. In the summer she meant to try all kinds of experiments. She had visions of rigging up a shelter made of leaves and branches, and taking a series of magnificent snap-shots of wild birds and animals, like those in the books by Cherry Kearton, and she certainly intended to secure records of the sports at school. In the meantime she must content herself with landscape and still life. "I'll have one of the de Claremont tomb, at any rate," she resolved.

The de Claremont tomb was the glory of Ashbourne Church. It was of white marble, and beautifully sculptured. Sir Guy de Claremont lay represented in full armor, with his lady in ruff and coif by her side. Six sons and four daughters, all kneeling, were carved in has relief round the side of the monument. Long, long ago, in the Middle Ages, the de Claremonts had been the great people of the neighborhood. They had fought in the Crusades, had taken their part in the wars of the Barons, had declared for the White Rose in the struggle with the House of Lancaster, and cast in their lot for the King against

Oliver Cromwell. The family was extinct now, and their lands had passed to others, but a few tattered banners and an old helmet still hung on the wall of the side chapel, above the tomb, testifying to their former achievements. From her seat in church Winona had a good view of the monument. She admired it immensely, and had often woven romances about the good knights of old who had carried those banners to the battle-field. She felt that she would like to secure a satisfactory photo. She started off one morning at about half-past eleven, when the light was likely to be best.

It was a sunny day, and wonderfully bright for January. She had meant to go alone, but the children were on the look-out, and tracked her, so she arrived at the church door closely followed by Letty, Mamie, Godfrey, Ernie and Dorrie. She hesitated for a moment whether to send them straight home or not, but the church was a mile from Highfield, and the mill weir, a place of fascination to Ernie, lay on the way, so she decided that it would be safest to let well alone.

"They're imps, but they'll have to behave themselves decently in church," she said to herself.

At present the conduct of the family was exemplary. They walked in on tip-toe, and talked in whispers. Mamie, indeed, cast an envious eye towards the forbidden ground of the pulpit, into which it was her ambition some day to climb, and wave her arms about in imitation of the Vicar, but she valiantly restrained her longings, and kept from the neighborhood of the chancel. Letty took a surreptitious peep at the organ, and was disappointed to find it locked, as was also the little oak door that led up the winding staircase to the bell tower. She decided that the parish clerk was much too attentive to his duties.

"Come along over here, can't you?" said Winona suspiciously. "Leave those hymn-books alone, and tell Dorrie she's not to touch the font, or I'll stick her inside and pop the lid on her. Go and sit down, all of you, in that pew, while I take the photo."

The family for once complied obediently, if somewhat reluctantly. It was better to play the part of spectators than to be left out of the proceedings altogether. In the circumstances they knew Winona had the whip-hand, and that if she ordered them from the church there would be no appeal. They watched her now with interest and enthusiasm.

It took her a long time to fix her camera in good position. It was difficult to see properly in the viewfinder, and she wanted to be quite sure that when the head of Sir Guy was safely in the right-hand corner, his feet were not out of the picture at the left, to say nothing of the ten kneeling children underneath.

"It's impossible to get the wall above if I'm to take the inscription on the monument," she declared, "and yet I mustn't leave out the old helmet on any account. I shall take it down, and put it at the bottom of the tomb while I photograph it. It ought to come out rather well there."

Rejecting eager offers of help from Mamie and Ernie, Winona climbed up on to the stately person of Dame Margaret de Claremont, and managed to take the helmet from the wooden peg on which it was suspended. She posed it at the foot of the monument, on the right hand side.

"There's a splendid light from this window - full sunshine! I think if I give it five minutes' exposure, that ought to do the deed. Now don't any of you so much as cough, or you'll disturb the air."

The family felt *that* five minutes the very limit of endurance. The moment it was ended they dispersed to ease their strained feelings. Letty and Ernie walked briskly up the nave. Mamie went to investigate the stove. Winona herself took the camera to the opposite side of the church to photograph a Jacobean tablet. Six-year-old Dorrie remained sitting on a hassock in the pew. She had a plan in her crafty young mind. She wanted to examine the helmet, and she knew Winona would be sure to say "Paws off!" or something equally offensive and objectionable. She waited till her sister was safely out of the way, then she stole from her cover, grabbed the helmet, and returned to the shelter of the pew. It made quite an interesting and fascinating plaything in her estimation. She amused herself with it for a long time, until she heard Winona's voice proclaiming that if they didn't trot home quickly they'd be late for dinner, whereupon she popped it under the seat, and joined the others. Winona, of course, ought to have replaced it on its peg on the wall, but her memory was far from perfect, and she completely forgot all about it.

The whole thing seemed a most trivial incident, but it had an amazing sequel. On Saturday afternoons Mrs. Fisher, the caretaker, always came to sweep and tidy up the church in preparation for Sunday. She was a little, thin, sharp-nosed, impulsive woman, and just at present her nerves were rather in a shaky condition for fear of Zeppelins. She lived in perpetual terror of bombs or German spies, and always slept with half her clothing on, in case she should be forced to get up in a hurry and flee for her life. On this particular Saturday afternoon Mrs. Fisher, as was her wont, washed the pavement of the nave, and then took her broom and her duster into the side chapel. Nobody sat there as a rule, so she did not give it very much attention. She flicked the duster over the monument, hastily swept the floor in front, and was just about to turn away, having done her duty, when she caught sight of something under the seat of a pew. She put her hand to her heart, and turned as white as her own best linen apron. She divined instantly what it must be. With great presence of mind she stole softly away on tip-toe. Once outside the church she indulged in a comfortable little burst of hysterics. Then she felt better, and went to tell the parish clerk. Before evening the news had spread all over the village.

"It was brought in a motor car," Mrs. Pikes at the shop informed her customers, "and Wilson's little boy says he heard them talking German."

"There was a foreign-looking sort of a chap rode past our house on a bicycle the other day," volunteered the blacksmith's assistant.

"You never know where you are with strangers in war time," said another.

Everybody agreed that it was a mercy Mrs. Fisher had seen it when she did, and they were glad the church was a goodish way from the village.

The Woodward family generally started off for service almost directly after the bells began to ring. On the following Sunday morning, however, they were considerably perplexed. The familiar "ding-dong, ding-dong" which ought to have been pealing forth was not to be heard. They listened in vain, and consulted all the clocks in the house.

"It's certainly after ten," said Mrs. Woodward. "I'm afraid something must have happened! I hope Mr. James isn't ill. Well, we'd better go at any rate, and see what's the matter."

So the family, which was ready in its best Sunday garments, sallied forth. Ashbourne Church stood a whole mile away from the village, in a lonely spot with only a couple of cottages near it. The Woodwards took a short cut across the common from Highfield, so that they did not pass any houses or meet any neighbors by the way. They arrived at the church to find the door locked, and the Vicar and his family standing in consternation outside. Mr. James hailed them with relief.

"So it *is* Sunday!" he exclaimed. "I began to think we must have mistaken the day! I can't understand what's the matter. Nobody's here except ourselves. What's becomes of Stevens?"

It was certainly an unprecedented circumstance to find choir, congregation, organist, organ-blower, bell-ringer and verger all conspicuous by their absence. Mr. James went to the cottages near to make inquiries as to the cause. The first was locked up, but by knocking long and loudly at the door of the second, he at last succeeded in rousing Jacob Johnson, a deaf old man of eighty-three.

"Nobody come to church!" he repeated, when after some difficulty and much shouting the situation had been explained: "Well, 'tain't likely there should be! I'm told there's a German bomb there, one of the dangerous sort for going off. Some men brought it yesterday in a motor car. Spies of the Kaiser, they were. It may explode any minute, they say, and wreck the church and everything near. The Greenwoods next door locked up the house, and went to their aunt's in the village. My daughter came over here asking me to go home with her, but I said I'd stay and risk it. At eighty-three one doesn't care to move!"

"Where is this bomb?" asked Mr. James.

"In a pew nigh the old monument, so I'm told." At this juncture Jack Cassidy, who when the church was first found to be locked had volunteered to run back to the Vicarage and fetch the Vicar's own key, now arrived after a record sprint.

"Give me a bucket of water, and I'll go and investigate," said Mr. James.

He came out of the church in the course of a few minutes, holding in his hand - the old helmet!

"This is the nearest approach to a bomb of any description that I've been able to discover," he announced. "I'm going to carry it to the village to convince the wiseacres there. Perhaps Stevens will pluck up courage to ring the bell for afternoon service. If not, I'll ring it myself."

Winona's share in the business might have remained concealed but for the indiscretion of Mamie, who by an incautious remark gave the show away entirely.

"You little silly!" scolded Winona afterwards. "What possessed you to go and say anything at all? Mr. James will never forgive me! I could see it in his eye. And Mrs. James was ice itself! I've never felt so horrible in all my life. If you'd only had the sense to keep mum, they might never have found out. You kids are the most frightful nuisance! If I'd had my choice given me when I was born, I wouldn't have been an eldest sister."

Angela Brazil

CHAPTER IX

THE SCHOOL SERVICE BADGE

Settling down at Abbey Close after a month at Highfield was like transferring oneself from a noisy farmyard to the calm of the cloister. The house was so near to the Minster that it seemed pervaded by the quiet Cathedral atmosphere. When Winona drew up her blinds in the morning, the first sight that greeted her would be the grey old towers and carved pinnacles, exactly opposite, where the jackdaws were chattering, and the pigeons wheeling round, and the big clock was going through the chimes and striking the hour of seven. There was a particular gargoyle at the corner of the transept roof which appeared to be grinning at her across the road, as if some imp were imprisoned in the stone image, and were peeping out of its fantastic eyes. Winona had grown to love the Minster. She would go in whenever she had ten minutes to spare after school. The glorious arches and pillars, the carved choir stalls, the light falling through the splendid rich windows on to the marble pavement, all appealed to the artistic sense that was stirring in her, and gave her immense satisfaction. But even the beauty of the Cathedral was as nothing when the organ began to play. Mr. Holmes, the organist, was a great musician, and could manage his instrument with a wizard touch. In the afternoons, between four and five o'clock, he was wont to practice his voluntaries, and to listen to these took Winona into a new world of sound. He was a disciple of the extreme modern school of music, and his interpretations of Debussy, Cesar Franck, Medtner and Glazounow came to her as a revelation. The glorious weird harmonies, the strange, unaccustomed chords of these tone-poems stirred her like the memory of something long forgotten. As Anglo-Indians, whose knowledge of Hindustani faded with their childhood, yet start and thrill at the sound of the once familiar language, so this dream-music brought haunting elusive suggestions too subtle to be defined. It held a distinct part in Winona's development.

The girl was growing up suddenly. In the almost nursery atmosphere of Highfield, with nothing to stimulate her faculties she had remained at a very childish stage, but now, with a world of art, music, science and literature dawning round her she seemed to leap upward to the level of her new intellectual horizon. It is a glorious time when we first begin to reap the inheritance of the ages, and to discover the rich stores of delight that master minds have laid up for us to enjoy. Life was moving very fast to Winona; she could not analyze all her fresh thoughts and impressions, but she felt she could no more go back to her last year's mental outlook than she could have worn the long clothes of her babyhood. She was sixteen now, for her birthday fell on the 20th of January. Somehow sixteen sounded so infinitely older than fifteen! There was a dignity about it and a sense of importance. In another year she would actually be "sweet seventeen," and a member of that enviable school hierarchy the Sixth Form!

Winona could have made herself thoroughly happy at Abbey Close but for the shadow that existed between herself and Aunt Harriet. Percy's secret was a perpetual burden on her conscience. At meal times she would often find her eyes wandering towards the oak cupboard, and would start guiltily, hoping Miss Beach had not noticed. The more she thought about the subject the more convinced she became that she ought to give some hint of the state of affairs, though how to do so without implicating her brother was at present beyond her calculations. One day, however, a really hopeful opportunity seemed to arise. A case of a disputed will was being tried at the Seaton Sessions; the defendants were friends of Miss

Beach's, and after reading the account of the proceedings, Aunt Harriet laid down the local paper with a few comments.

"I suppose people ought to make their wills very fast and firm," said Winona. It was seldom she ventured on an independent remark. As a rule she left her aunt to do the talking.

"Undoubtedly. Nothing causes more trouble than carelessness in this respect."

"Ought we all to make wills?"

"If we have anything to leave it's advisable."

"Ought I?"

"Well, hardly at present, I should say!"

"Ought mother?" Winona was growing redder and redder.

"No doubt she has done so."

"Have you made yours, Aunt Harriet?"

The horrible deed was done, and Winona, crimson to the roots of her hair, felt she had, metaphorically speaking, burnt her boats.

Miss Beach stared at her as if electrified.

"What do you want to know for?" she asked, suspiciously. "I think that's decidedly my business and not yours!"

Winona collapsed utterly, and murmuring something about preparation, fled to her bedroom.

"There! I've just gone and put my foot in it altogether!" she groaned. "I've no tact! I went and blurted it out like an idiot. She'll never forgive me! Oh, why can't I go and tell her the whole business, and then she'd understand! I do hate this sneaking work. Percy, you wretched boy, I'd like to bump your head against the wall! It's too bad to land me in your scrape! Well, I suppose it can't be helped. I've said it, and it's done. But I know I'll be in disgrace for evermore."

Certainly Aunt Harriet's manner towards Winona, after this unfortunate episode, was stiffer than formerly. She was perfectly kind, but the gulf between them had widened. They still discussed conventional topics at meal-times, or rather Miss Beach made leading remarks and Winona said "Yes," or "No," for such a one-sided conversation could hardly be termed discussion. The girl felt it a relief when, as often happened, her aunt took refuge in a book. Occasionally Winona would pluck up courage to relate news from her home letters, but of her school life and all her new impressions and interests she scarcely spoke at all. Judging from the children's correspond-ence the new governess at Highfield, after a stormy beginning, was making some impressions upon her wild little pupils.

"I hated her at first," wrote Mamie, "but she tells us the most lovely fairy tales, and we're learning to model in clay. I like it because it makes such a mess. Ernie smacked her yesterday, and she wouldn't let him do his painting till he'd said he was sorry."

Winona laughed over the letters, picturing the lively scenes that must be taking place at home.

"Do the kids a world of good!" she commented. "They were running to seed. Even I could see that, as long ago as last summer, and I don't mind confessing, quite to myself, that I was fairly raw then. I didn't know very much about anything till I came to the 'Seaton High.'"

Winona's second term was running far more smoothly than her first. Thanks to Miss Lever's coaching she could now hold her own in her Form, and though she might not be the most shining light, at any rate she was not numbered among

Angela Brazil

the slackers.

Her progress was marked in more quarters than she suspected. Margaret Howell had had the Scholarship winners under observation ever since their arrival. As head girl she made it her business to know something about every girl in the school. "The General," as she was nicknamed, was universally voted a success. She and Kirsty Paterson between them had organized a new era of things. Every one felt the "Seaton High" was waking up and beginning to found a reputation for itself. The various guilds and societies were prospering, and following Margaret's pet motto "Pro Bono Publico," had exterminated private quarrels and instituted the most business-like proceedings and the strictest civility at committee meetings. Already the general tone was raised immeasurably, and public spirit and school patriotism ran high. To encourage zeal and strenuousness, Margaret and Kirsty had laid their heads together and decided to found what they called "The Order of Distinguished School Service." Any girl who was considered to have performed some action worthy of special commendation or who had otherwise contributed to the general benefit, was to be rewarded with a badge, and her name was to be chronicled in a book kept for the purpose.

The very first to gain the honor was little Daisy Hicks, a Second Form child, who won 9,400 marks out of a possible 10,000 in the Christmas exams, so far the highest score known in the school. Agnes Heath, who wrung special praise from the doctor who conducted the Ambulance examination, and Gladys Vickcrs, whose photograph of the hockey team was published in the Seaton *Weekly Graphic*, were also placed upon the distinguished list, having substantially helped the credit of the school. The badge was only a rosette made of narrow ribbons, stitched in tiny loops into the form of a daisy, with a yellow disk, and white and pink outer rays. If meant very much, however, to the recipient, who knew that her name would be handed down to posterity in the school traditions, and every girl was immensely keen to earn it.

A new institution in the school this term was the foundation of a library. It had been a pet project of Margaret's ever since her appointment as head prefect. Just before the Christmas breaking up she had called a general meeting and begged everybody after the holidays to present at least one contribution.

"It may be a new book or an old one," she had explained, "but it must be really interesting. Please don't bring rubbish. Give something you would enjoy reading yourself and can recommend to your friends."

The response to her appeal had been greater than she anticipated. Nobody failed to comply, and some of the girls brought several books apiece. A start was made with three hundred and forty-one volumes, which was regarded as a most creditable beginning. For the present they were piled up in the prefects' room until shelves had been made to receive them. Miss Bishop had given the order to the joiner, but owing to the war it might be some time before the work was finished.

Meanwhile Margaret decided that the books ought to be catalogued and labeled, so that they would be quite ready when the bookcases arrived. She cast about for helpers in this rather arduous task, and her choice fell upon Winona, who happened to have a spare half-hour between her classes on Tuesday and Thursday afternoons. Winona, immensely flattered, accepted the responsibility with glee, and was put to work under the "General's" directions. She thoroughly enjoyed sorting, dusting, pasting on labels, and making alphabetical lists.

"I shouldn't mind being a librarian some day in a big public library," she assured Ellinor Cooper, her fellow-assistant.

"You'd have to be quicker than you are at present, then," remarked Margaret dryly. "They wouldn't think you worth your salt if you spent all your time reading the books. Buck up, can't you? and get on!"

At which Winona guiltily shut "Shirley" with a bang and turned her attention to the paste-pot.

While Margaret was cultivating the intellectual side of the school, Kirsty was carefully attending to her duties as Games Captain. Her work among the juniors prospered exceedingly. They were taking to hockey with wild enthusiasm and gave evidence of considerable promise. As most of them were free at three o'clock, they got the chance of playing almost every day. Kirsty was extremely anxious that these practices should be properly supervised. She was too busy herself to take them personally, so she was obliged to delegate the work to anybody who had the spare time.

"The girls I want most are all at classes or music lessons," she lamented. "Not a single one of the team's available. Winona Woodward, I've been looking at your time-table, and find you've two vacant half-hours. Wouldn't you like to help?"

"Like! I'd sell my birthright to do it!" gasped Winona. "But I'm fearfully sorry; I'm cataloguing for Margaret!"

"Then I mustn't take you away from the General! It's a nuisance though, for you'd have done very well, and I don't know who else I can get."

Winona considered it was one of the sharpest disappointments she had ever gone through.

"Oh, the grizzly bad luck of it!" she wailed to Garnet. "It would have been idyllic to coach those kids. And it would have given me such a leg up with Kirsty! To think I've lost my chance!"

"I suppose Margaret might get some one else to do cataloguing?"

"I dare say: but I couldn't possibly ask her, and I'm sure Kirsty won't. No, I'm done for!"

School etiquette is very strict, and Winona would have perished sooner than resign her library duties. She felt a martyr, but resolved to smile through it all. Garnet contemplated the problem at leisure during her drawing lesson, and arrived at a daring conclusion. Without consulting her friend she marched off at four o'clock to the prefects' room, a little sanctum on the ground floor where the minutes' books of the various guilds and societies were kept, and where the school officers could hold meetings and transact business.

As she expected, Margaret was there alone, and said "Come in" in answer to her rap at the door. The members of the Sixth kept much on their dignity, so it was rather a formidable undertaking even for a Fifth Form girl to interrupt the head of the school. Margaret looked up inquiringly as Garnet entered.

"Yes, I'm fearfully busy," she replied to the murmured question. "What is it? I can give you five minutes, but no more, so please be brief."

Thus urged, Garnet, though greatly embarrassed, did not beat about the bush.

"I've come to ask a frightfully cheeky thing," she blurted out. "Kirsty wants Winona to coach the kids at hockey, and Winona's cataloguing for you, so of course she can't - and -" but here Garnet's courage failed her, so she paused.

"Do you mean that Winona would prefer to help with the juniors?"

"She'd be torn in pieces rather than let me say so, but she's just crazy over hockey. I hope I haven't made any mischief! Win doesn't know I've come."

"All right. I understand. I'll see what can be done in the matter," returned the General, opening her books as a sign of dismissal.

Garnet was not at all sure whether her mission had succeeded or the reverse, but the next day Margaret sent for Winona.

"I hear Kirsty wants you for a hockey coach. Just at present I think games are of more importance in the school than the library, so please report yourself to her, and say I've taken your name off my list. You've done very well here, but I'm going to lend you to Kirsty for a while."

Winona was so astounded she hardly knew whether to stammer out apologies, gratitude, or regrets, and was intensely relieved when the head girl cut her short kindly but firmly, and sent her away. She lost no time in seeking out the Games Captain.

"Very decent of Margaret," remarked Kirsty. "It's got me out of a hole, for I couldn't find anybody else with that special time free. You'll do your best I know?"

"*Rather*!" beamed Winona ecstatically.

Under her tuition the children's play improved fast. Kirsty said little - she was not given to over-praising people - but Winona felt she noticed and approved.

Among the season's fixtures perhaps the most important was the match with the Seaton Ladies' Hockey Club that was to come off on March 7th. Their opponents possessed a fair reputation in the city, so it would behove the school to "play up for all they were worth," as Kirsty expressed it. It would be a glorious opportunity of showing their capabilities to the world at large, and demonstrating that they meant to take their due place in local athletics.

Three days before the event, Kirsty appeared in the morning with the air of a tragedy queen.

"What's the matter?" queried Patricia. "You've a face as long as a fiddle!"

"Matter enough! Barbara Jennings is laid up with influenza! What'll become of the match I don't know. It makes me feel rocky. Where's Margaret? I want to confab. Did you ever hear of such grizzly luck in your life?"

At five minutes past eleven, when Winona was eating her lunch in the gymnasium, Kirsty tapped her on the shoulder.

"I've something to tell you, Winona Woodward. You're to play for the School on Saturday instead of Barbara."

Winona swallowed a piece of biscuit with foolhardy haste. She could scarcely believe the news, so great was its magnitude. To be asked to fill a vacant place in the team was beyond her wildest dreams.

"Thanks most *immensely*!" she stammered, with her eyes shining like stars.

Through the next few days Winona simply lived for Saturday. To be able to represent the School! The glorious thought was never for a moment absent from her mind. She even ventured to tell Aunt Harriet the honor that had been thrust upon her, and was astonished at the interest with which her information was received.

On the Saturday afternoon the High School turned up almost in full force to view the match; juniors were keen as seniors, and the children whom Winona had coached were wild with excitement. The field was packed with spectators, for the Ladies' Club had brought many friends. It was even rumored that a reporter from the Seaton *Weekly Graphic* was present. The High School team in navy blue gymnasium costumes, bare heads and close-plaited pigtails, looked neat and trim and very business-like. "A much fitter set than we showed last year!" murmured Margaret with satisfaction. All eyes were riveted on the field as the two opponents stood out to "bully" and the sticks first clashed together. Winona, her face aglow with excitement, waited a chance to run. A little later her opportunity came: she dashed into the masses of the opponents' force, and with one magnificent stroke swept the ball well onward towards the goal.

"Oh! how precious!" shouted the girls.

Nobody had imagined Winona capable of such a feat. She at once became the focus of all eyes. It had not occurred to the High School that there was a real possibility of their winning the match. They had expected to make a gallant fight and be defeated, retiring with all the honors of war. Perhaps the Ladies' Club team, who had come to the field secure of victory, began to feel pangs of uneasiness under their white jerseys. The situation was supreme. The score had become even. Could the School possibly do it? That was the question. All looked to Winona for the answer. She was playing like one inspired. She had not realized her own capacities before: the wild excitement of the moment seemed to lend wings to her feet and strength and skill to her arm. One heroic, never-to-be-forgotten stroke, and the ball was spinning between the posts. It was a magnificent finish. Frantic applause rose up from the spectators. The High School cheered its champions in a glorious roar of victory. The Ladies' Club team were magnanimous enough to offer congratulations, and their captain shook hands with Winona.

"Glad to see how your standard's gone up!" she remarked to Kirsty aside. "That half-back of yours is worth her salt!"

Kirsty was literally purring with satisfaction. Last year the High School had been badly beaten in more than half its matches. This was indeed a new page in its records.

On Monday morning Winona received a message summoning her to the prefects' room. She found Margaret, Kirsty, and the other school officers assembled there.

"Winona Woodward," said the head girl, "we have decided to present you with the School Service Badge, in recognition of your play on Saturday. It is felt that you really secured the match, and as this is our first great victory we consider you deserve to have it recorded in your favor. Your name has been entered in the book. Come here!"

Winona turned crimson as Margaret pinned the daisy badge on to her blouse.

"I - I've been only too proud to do what I can!" she blurted out. "Thanks most *awfully!*"

CHAPTER X

A SCARE

The Spring Term came to a close with a very fair number of hockey successes to be placed to the credit of the Seaton High School. Compared with last year's record it was indeed a great improvement, and Kirsty felt that though they had not yet established a games reputation, they at any rate showed good promise of future achievements. She hoped to do much in the cricket and tennis season, though she certainly acknowledged there was much to be done. The cricket so far had been such a half-hearted business that she doubted the advisability of making any fixtures.

"I believe we'd just better train up for all we're worth," she said at the committee meeting. "It'll take ages to lick an eleven into shape. What we want is to get a cricket atmosphere into the school. You can't develop these things all in a few weeks. You've got to catch your kids young and teach them, before you get a school with a reputation. I feel with all the games that we're simply building foundations at present at the Seaton High. This term especially is spade-work. I'll do all I can to get things going, but it will be the Games Captain who comes after me who'll reap the reward."

"Can't you stay on another year?" suggested Patricia.

"Wish I could for some things, but it's impossible. No, I'll do my bit this term, and then hand over the job to my successor.

As I said before, what we want now is a good start."

Kirsty was a capital organizer. She soon recognized a girl's capacities, and she had a knack of inspiring enthusiasm even in apparent slackers. She worked thoroughly hard herself, and insisted that everybody else did the same. Her motto for the term was the athletic education of the rank and file. It was really very self-sacrificing of her, for she might have gained far more credit by concentrating her energies on a few, but for the ultimate good of the school it was undoubtedly far and away the best policy to pursue. The training of a number of recruits may not be as interesting as the polishing up of champions, but in time recruits become veterans, and a school in which the standard of the ordinary play is very high has a better general chance than one that depends on an occasional *solitary* star. So even the little girls were strictly supervised in their practices, and both cricket and tennis showed healthy development.

The Governors and the head mistress were anxious that the games department should prosper, and gave every encouragement. There were a larger number of tennis courts provided than fall to the share of most schools, and each form had its allotted times for play. Athletics were indeed compulsory, every girl being required to take her due part, unless she were excused by a medical certificate.

Winona worked with the utmost enthusiasm. As a Fifth Form girl she had, of course, to be rather humble towards the Sixth, but she felt that Kirsty approved of her. It was never Kirsty's way to praise, and she could be scathing in her remarks sometimes, but Winona did not mind criticism from her captain, and acted so well on all the advice given that she was making rapid strides. In pursuance of Kirsty's all-round training policy, she was not allowed to specialize in either tennis or cricket this summer, but to give equal energy to both. So she practiced bowling under Hester King's careful supervision, and played exciting sets while Clarice Nixon stood by to watch and score.

The games appealed to Winona more than any other part of the school curriculum. She did fairly well now in her Form work, but she knew she could never be clever like Garnet, and that it was extremely unlikely that she would win laurels on her books. She had promised Miss Bishop that she would try to do credit to the school in return for her scholarship, and to help to raise its athletic reputation seemed her most feasible method of success.

"I could never get a College Scholarship, however I tried," she thought, "but - I won't say it's probable, but it's just possible that I might do something some day in the way of winning matches. Miss Bishop would be pleased at that!"

The early summer was delightful at Seaton. The park opposite the school was full of tulips and hyacinths, and the long avenue of trees in the Abbey Close had burst into tender green foliage. Winona studied her home lessons sitting by her open bedroom window with a leafy bower outside, and an accompaniment of jackdaws cawing in the old towers of the Minster. She loved this window and the prospect from it. There was a romantic, old-world flavor about the gray pile opposite, its carvings and cloisters and chiming bells seemed so peaceful and so far removed from modern trouble. Sometimes indeed the whirr of a biplane would disturb the quiet as an airman flittered like a great dragon-fly over the city, reminding her that medieval times were past; while a bugle call from the neighboring barracks emphasized the fact that the world was at war. Not that Winona was likely to forget that! Every day in school the Peace Bell prayer was read at noon, and she might see regiments of recruits marching up or down the High Street on their way to their training grounds. Nearly every girl in V.a. had some relation at the front, and though Winona could not boast of anybody nearer than a third cousin serving "somewhere in France," she looked for news as eagerly as the rest.

"It must be glorious to get letters from the trenches," she said half wistfully one day to Beatrice Howell, who was exulting over a pencil scrawl written by her brother in a dug-out. "I half wish -"

"No, you don't!" snapped Beatrice. "It's a nightmare to have them in the firing line! Be thankful your brother's still safe at school."

On the subject of Percy, Winona was far from easy. He had let fall one or two hints during the Easter holidays which confirmed her previous suspicion that he had got into a wrong set at Longworth College. He had written to her twice already this term, wanting to borrow money, and suggesting that, without mentioning his name, she should ask Miss Beach to lend it to her. With such a request, however, Winona had utterly refused to comply.

"Aunt Harriet has been so decent to us I can't begin to sponge on her," she wrote back. "Besides, she'd want to know what I wanted such a lot for, and then all the mischief would be out!"

Apparently Percy was offended, for his usual weekly letter did not appear. Winona only laughed, expecting he would soon get over his fit of sulks. She was utterly unprepared for the sequel. One day she received a note from him written on Y.M.C.A. paper and headed "Horminster." It ran thus:

> "DEAR WIN, - I'd got into such an altogether grizzly hole that there was only one way out, and I've taken it. I am at present a member of His Majesty's Forces, and if you want to write to me address: Private P. D. Woodward, 17th Battalion, Royal Rytonshire Fusiliers, Horminster.
>
> "Your affectionate brother,
>
> "PERCY."
>
> "P.S. - You can tell the mater if you like."

Winona, in a great state of excitement, showed the note to Aunt Harriet, who telegraphed the information to Mrs.

Woodward. The latter had just heard from Percy's house-master of his disappearance, and was greatly relieved to have news of his whereabouts. The runaway was below military age, and his mother's first impulse was to apply for his immediate discharge. But from this course her best friends dissuaded her. The headmaster of Longworth College and Mr. Joynson, her trustee, were unanimous in counseling her to leave the boy alone, and Aunt Harriet cordially agreed with them.

"Let the lad serve his country!" she wrote to her niece. "He is tall for his age, and if the Military Authorities have accepted him, well and good. It seems to me the one thing in the world that is likely to steady him and give him that sense of responsibility that hitherto he has so signally lacked. You will make the mistake of your life if you keep him back now."

It seemed funny to Winona to imagine Percy, so young and boyish, actually in His Majesty's uniform. He had not yet got his khaki, but he promised to have a photo taken as soon as ever he was in military garb, and she looked forward to showing the portrait of her soldier brother to the girls in her Form. She began a pair of socks for him at once. I regret to say that Winona's patriotic knitting had languished very much during the last two terms, but this personal stimulus revived her ardor. She even took her sock to the tennis court, and, emulating the example of Patricia Marshall and several other enthusiasts, got quite good pieces done between the sets. She would have taken it to cricket also, but Kirsty had sternly made a by-law prohibiting all knitting on the pitch since Ellinor Cooper, when supposed to be fielding, had surreptitiously taken her work from her pocket and missed the best catch of the afternoon, to her everlasting disgrace and the scorn of the indignant Games Captain.

Kirsty was keen at present upon each Form having its own Eleven, and had arranged some school matches as trials of skill. The first of these, Sixth v. Fifth, was fixed for the following Saturday afternoon. Winona, to her ecstatic and delirious delight, had been elected captain of the combined V.a. and

V.b. Eleven, and she was looking forward to the contest as one of the events of her life. She was aware that on its success or failure might hang much of her future athletic career at school, and she was determined to show of what stuff she was made. She urged her team to make heroic efforts, and got all the practice in that was available. On the Thursday afternoon she gave everybody a final drilling. On Friday the pitch would be the property of the Lower School, so this was the last opportunity of play before the match.

"If any of you muff the ball or do anything stupid, I'll never forgive you!" she assured her Eleven. "The Sixth are A1 at fielding, so for goodness' sake don't disgrace our Form. Beware of Patricia's bowling. It looks simple, but it's the nastiest I know. I'd rather have Kirsty's any day, because at least you know what to expect from her, and you're on your guard. Don't try to be clever too soon; it's better not to score at all during the first over than to run any risks. Evelyn, you were a mascot to-day! I hope you'll play up equally well on Saturday. By the by, Joyce, I really can't compliment you on your innings. What were you thinking of to make that idiotic blind swipe?"

"I don't know!" returned Joyce dolefully. (She was sitting on the fence looking decidedly crestfallen.) "I'm afraid I'm rather rocky to-day, somehow."

"Got nerves? Girl alive! Do brace up!"

"No, it's not nerves. My head's been aching all the week, and I've a pain across my chest, and I keep shivering. I suppose I must have caught cold. It'll be a grizzly nuisance if I can't play on Saturday!"

"You *must* play!" urged Winona. "We've got to beat the Sixth or perish in the attempt! You go home at once, and get some hot tea, and go to bed afterwards if you don't feel better. You may stop in bed all to-morrow if it'll do you good!"

"Thank you, Grannie! Perhaps I will go home now. I really am feeling rather queer."

"She looks queer, too," said Bessie Kirk to Winona, as they stood watching Joyce's retreating figure. "I thought she was going to faint a while ago. It'll be a hideous nuisance if she has to be out of it."

"Our best bowler! It's unthinkable!" groaned Winona.

"It's hard luck, but I'm certain Joyce won't play on Saturday," said Mary Payne.

The team was feeling rather down at the prospect.

"We may throw up the sponge if Joyce is off!" mourned Olave Parry.

"Shut up, you bluebottle!" snapped Winona, decidedly out of temper. "Joyce may be absolutely well again by Saturday, and if she isn't Marjorie Kemp must take her place. Do be sporting! You'll never win if you make up your mind beforehand that you're going to lose!"

When Winona walked into *V.a.* on the following morning she looked anxiously in the direction of Joyce's desk, but the familiar check dress and amber pigtail were not to be seen. Little groups of girls were standing in clusters, talking in apparent consternation.

"Well! Have you heard the news?" asked Garnet, stepping forward to meet her friend.

"No. What's the damage? You're looking very down in the dumps!"

"Joyce Newton has developed small-pox!"

"Nonsense!" exploded Winona.

"It's perfectly true," said Garnet, with severe dignity in her voice. "One only wishes for Joyce's sake that it wasn't! The news has only just come. Helena Maitland knows about it. She lives next door, and saw the doctor's car at the Newtons' gate this morning."

"I told you Joyce looked queer yesterday!" said Bessie Kirk.

"Suppose we all catch it!" shuddered Freda Long.

"Don't! It's too horrible!"

There was a feeling of utter consternation among the girls as the bad news was discussed. They wondered what was going to happen.

"Miss Bishop is telephoning to the Medical Officer of Health," volunteered Olave Parry, who had been downstairs to seek fresh information.

Just then Miss Huntley came into the room, though it was not yet nine o'clock. She went at once to her desk and took the call over.

"What's going to happen about Joyce?" one or two of the girls ventured to ask her.

"I don't know yet. I expect we shall all be put into quarantine. Miss Bishop is making arrangements. In the meantime we will go on with our work."

It was wise of Miss Huntley to begin the English Language lesson, for though every one was of course very abstracted, it gave some ostensible occupation. Before the hour was over Miss Bishop sailed into the room. She looked pale and anxious, but spoke with her usual calm dignity.

"Girls," she announced, "you have heard of the very difficult situation in which the school is placed. I have rung up Dr.

Barnes, the Medical Officer of Health, and he tells me that the whole of *V.a.* must be regarded as 'contact cases.' That means that as Joyce has been amongst you, it is possible for any of you to develop the disease. In order to avoid the spread of infection throughout the city, you will have to be most carefully kept apart. I have sent all the other girls home, and you will stay at the school during to-day. Dr. Barnes is coming this morning to re-vaccinate you, and this afternoon you are to be taken to the Camp at Dunheath, where you will stay until the period of quarantine is over. Go home? Most certainly not! No girl is to leave the school on any pretext whatever. I am communicating with your home people and requesting that they send you a few necessary things to take to the camp, but no personal interviews can be allowed. Dr. Barnes' orders are most emphatic. You need not be alarmed, for if you are all re-vaccinated it is highly improbable that you will be infected, and I think you will all enjoy yourselves at Dunheath."

When the Principal had gone the girls clustered round Miss Huntley to discuss the situation.

"Yes, of course I'm going with you," said the mistress. "I'm a contact case as much as anybody else! Miss Bishop tells me that Dr. Barnes will send a hospital nurse with us. It's a nuisance to be in quarantine, but it will be beautiful out in the country just now, and we'll manage to enjoy ourselves."

The girls took the matter in various fashions according to their respective temperaments. Some were nervous, while others regarded it as a joke. The latter rallied their more timorous companions with scant mercy.

"Oh, buck up, you sillies!" said Marjorie Kemp, to the tearful plaints of Agatha James and Irene Mills. "Vaccination doesn't hurt! It's nothing but a scratch. You might be going to have your arms cut off. For goodness' sake show some pluck! Suppose you were in the trenches? The Camp will be just topping. We'll have the time of our lives!"

"If we don't break out in spots!" wailed Irene.

"Well, wait till you do before you make a fuss. You're far more likely to catch a thing if you're afraid of it."

"Oh, I say!" said Winona, suddenly remembering Saturday's event. "The match to-morrow will be all off!"

"Hold me up! So it will! What a grizzly nuisance! Oh, the hard luck of it!"

"Well, it can't be helped! We must play the Sixth later on."

"Kirsty'll be as savage as we are!"

"Poor old Joyce, she's responsible for a good deal of damage!"

The rest of the day passed in an extraordinary fashion. V.a. had the whole of the school premises absolutely and entirely to itself. The Fourth Form room was turned into a temporary surgery, and Dr. Barnes installed himself there with tubes of vaccine and packets of new darning needles. Each girl in turn went first to Miss Bishop and had her arm thoroughly sterilized with boiled water and boracic lotion, and was then passed on to the medical officer for vaccination. The scratch with the needle really did not hurt, and the little operations were soon over. Sixteen maidens walking about waiting for their arms to dry before re-donning their blouses made a rather comical sight. The giggles that ensued raised the spirits of even Agatha and Irene.

"Glad it was done on our left arms! I expect we sha'n't be in much form for cricket after this, unless we play one-handed!" laughed Winona. "By the by, will there be any field we can practice on out at the camp?"

"I expect so," returned Miss Huntley. "You had better make a collection of bats, balls and stumps and a few tennis rackets, and also your school books. Put them all together, and Miss Bishop will have them sent to us."

The girls hastened to sort out the necessary impedimenta for cricket and tennis, but arranged piles of books with less enthusiasm, the general opinion being that it was rather stiff to be expected to do work at the Camp. They were each allowed to take a book from the school library, and Miss Huntley added a pile of foolscap paper, pens and a big bottle of ink, which the girls devoutly hoped might get broken on the way and thus save them the labor of writing exercises. They had dinner and a four o'clock tea at school, after which meal Miss Bishop, who seemed to have spent most of the day at the telephone, announced that arrangements were now completed, and that they must get ready to start. Great was the excitement when at five o'clock a motor char-a-banc made its appearance. The sixteen "contacts" and Miss Huntley took their places, their hand-bags, which had been sent from their respective homes during the course of the day, were stowed away with the rest of their luggage inside a motor 'bus, and the company, feeling much more like a picnic party than possibly infected cases, drove merrily away for their period of quarantine.

CHAPTER XI

THE OPEN-AIR CAMP

If this particular Friday had been an exciting day to the girls of V.a., it had certainly proved a most agitating one to the Medical Officer of Health for Seaton. Upon his energy and organization depended the prevention of a serious epidemic in the city, and he had shown himself admirably able to cope with the sudden emergency. The Corporation had lately set up a camp for children threatened with tuberculosis, and this was commandeered by Dr. Barnes as a suitable place for quarantine. It lay five miles away from Seaton, on the top of a hill in a very open situation in the midst of fields, so was excellently fitted for the purpose. The children under treatment there had been hurriedly taken back to their homes in Seaton, extra beds and supplies had been sent out, and a hospital nurse installed in charge, so that all was in readiness when the char-a-banc arrived.

The Camp consisted of a long wooden shelter or shed, the south side of which was entirely open to the air. The boarded floor was raised about three feet above the level of the field, and projected well beyond the roof line, thus forming a kind of terrace. Inside the shelter was a row of small beds, and a space was curtained off at either end, on one side for a kitchen and on the other to make a cubicle for Miss Huntley. Outside, under a large oak tree, stood a table and benches. Nothing could have been more absolutely plain and bare as regards furniture. The girls took possession, however, with the utmost

Angela Brazil

enthusiasm. The idea of "living the simple life" appealed to them. Who wanted chairs and chests of drawers and wash-stands? It would be fun to sleep in the shelter, and spend the whole day out of doors.

"It's too topping for anything!" declared Marjorie Kemp, after a careful inspection of the premises. "We shall have to keep all our things inside our bags, and wash in an enameled tin basin, and drink our tea out of mugs!"

"It will be precious having meals under that tree!" agreed Bessie Kirk.

"What shall we do if it rains?" inquired Irene Mills.

"Go to bed with hot bottles, like the children did," replied Nurse Robinson. "They always thought that prime fun, so I expect you will too. You'll soon get into the life here."

The view from the shelter was most beautiful. In the far away distance they could see the towers of Seaton Minster and the spires of the churches, while all around lay lush meadows, fields of growing corn, and woods in the glory of June foliage. The Camp stood in the corner of a very large pasture, with hedges all covered with lovely wild roses and tangles of honeysuckle, while a wood close by showed a tempting vista of pine trees. The fresh country air and the smell of flowers and pines were delicious.

Life at the Camp was arranged according to a strict time-table. Every one rose at seven, and a certain number of volunteers helped to prepare breakfast. Then came bed-making, crockery washing and potato peeling, at which duties the girls took turns. From 9.30 to 12.30 they had classes with Miss Huntley, while Nurse Robinson superintended the cooking of the dinner on the large oil stove. With the exception of an hour's preparation the rest of the day was free from lessons. Tea was at four and supper at seven, and by half-past nine every one was in bed, well covered with blankets, and with a hot bottle if she liked, for the nights were apt to be chilly to those unaccustomed to sleeping in the open-air. The rules of quarantine were of course sternly kept. No girl might go outside the pasture without special permission. Sometimes Miss Huntley took her flock for a walk along quiet country roads and rambling by-lanes, but the vicinity of their fellow-creatures was carefully avoided.

"We're like the lepers in the Middle Ages!" laughed Garnet. "I feel as if I ought to wear a coarse white cassock, and ring a bell as I go about, to warn people to give me a wide berth!"

"It's amusing that the farmer has even driven his cows out of the pasture since we arrived," said Evelyn. "He let them feed here while the tuberculous children had their innings, and I should have thought consumption germs were as bad as small-pox ones."

"They weren't real consumptives though, only threatened!"

"Well, we're not small-pox patients, either, only contacts!"

"I'm sorry for those poor kids, sent suddenly back to their slum homes after being here for weeks," said Jess Gardner.

"Oh, the kids have had luck! There were only ten of them, and a lady at Hawberry has rigged up a tent in her garden, and has them all there, so Nurse told me this morning. They're living on the fat of the land, and gaining pounds and pounds in weight, by the look of them."

"Good! I don't feel so bad at having turned them out, then. It's great here!"

"Rather! On the whole, I feel thoroughly grateful to Joyce."

From the girls' point of view there really was matter for congratulation. None of them was ill, and all were having a most delightful and quite unexpected three weeks' holiday in idyllic surroundings. Their arms, to be sure, had "taken," and were more or less sore, but that was a trifling inconvenience compared with the pleasures of living in Camp. There was no anxiety to be felt about Joyce, she had the disease very slightly, and was being treated with such extreme care that her face would not be marked afterwards. It was ascertained that she had caught the infection from some Belgians who had come over lately from Holland, and who were now isolated by Dr. Barnes in a Cottage Hospital. The Seaton High School was undergoing elaborate disinfection, and as June was well advanced, the Governors had decided not to re-open until September, when all possibility of contagion would have passed away. This was the only part of the proceedings that did not please the girls.

"It's rather sickening to have no end to the term," groaned Marjorie. "Our matches are all off, and no swimming display or sports. It's rough on Margaret and Kirsty particularly. Do you realize that when we go back in September they'll both have left? All the prefects are leaving."

"Oh, hard luck! Who'll take their places?"

"Some of our noble selves, I suppose, if we're promoted to the Sixth."

"Who'll be General and Games Captain?"

"Ah! Ask me a harder, my intelligent child."

"I think I could put my finger on one of them, at any rate."

"So could I, perhaps, but I don't care to prophesy too soon," sighed Bessie.

Whoever might be destined to wear future laurels at school, Winona, as Captain of the V.a. team, assumed direction of the games at the Camp. Part of the pasture was sufficiently level to make quite a fair cricket pitch, while a piece in the opposite corner served as a tennis court. An old man from the farm was bribed to come and cut the grass with a scythe, but as no lawn-mower or roller was available, the result was decidedly rough. The tennis enthusiasts rigged up a tape in lieu of a net, and marked some courts with lime begged from the farmer. Their games, owing to the general bumpiness of the ground, had at least the charm of variety and excitement, and four umpires had to keep careful and continual watch in order to decide whether the balls went over or under the tape, which indeed collapsed occasionally, as the poles were only sticks cut from the hedge.

If the tennis was funny, the cricket was even funnier. Many of the girls could not use their left arms at all, consequently the batting was extraordinary, and sometimes the easiest catches were missed. It was very amusing, however, and perhaps for that reason provided more entertainment than the most strict and orthodox play under the critical eye of Kirsty might have done.

Really the quarantine party had a most idyllic time. In the warm June weather it was delightful to live out of doors. There were rosy-violet dawns and golden-red sunsets, and clear starry nights when the planet Venus shone like a lamp in the dark blue of the sky, and owls would fly hooting from the woods, and bats come flitting round the shelter in search of moths. One day, indeed, was wet, but the girls sat or lay on their beds, and read or talked, and played games, with intervals of exciting dashes in mackintoshes to fetch cans of water, or dishes from the larder.

On Sundays there was of course no church-going, but Miss Huntley read morning prayers, and in the evening they sang hymns, each girl in turn choosing the one she liked best. "All things bright and beautiful," "Nearer, my God, to Thee," and "Now the day is over" were prime favorites, but perhaps the most popular of all was the ancient Hymn of St. Patrick, which Miss Huntley had copied from a book of Erse literature, and had adapted to an old Irish tune. The girls learnt it easily, and its fifth century Celtic mysticism fascinated them. They liked such bits as:

"In light of sun, in gleam of snow
Myself I bind;
In speed of lightning, in depth of sea
In swiftness of wind.
God's Might to uphold me,
God's Wisdom to guide,
God's shield to protect me
In desert and wild."

* * *

"Christ with me, before me,
Behind me and in me,
O Threeness in Oneness
I praise and adore Thee."

"In Ireland it is sometimes called the Shamrock Hymn," said Miss Huntley, "because St. Patrick used the little green shamrock leaf to explain to the chiefs the doctrine of the Holy Trinity. The original is in a very ancient dialect of the Irish Celtic, and was preserved in an old manuscript book written on parchment. It always reminds me of the 'Benedicite omnia opera' of our prayer-book; the thought is the same in both: 'O ye spirits and souls of the righteous, bless ye the Lord' is about the sum of it all."

Except for the trifling trouble of vaccination, the effects of which in most cases were soon over, the quarantine party enjoyed radiant health. Dr. Barnes came twice a week to inspect, and Nurse Robinson kept a vigilant watch for head-aches, back-aches, and sickness. None of these symptoms appeared, however, and all began to congratulate themselves that the infection had been avoided. There was a burst of warm weather at the beginning of July, which made the hill breezes of Dunheath highly acceptable. It was too hot during the daytime to play active games; the girls lounged about under the shade of the trees, and read the illustrated papers with which they were kept plentifully supplied.

"I've never really had time before to study the toilet hints," said Beatrice Howell one afternoon, poring over a certain page headed "My Lady's Boudoir." "It seems to me that we ought to take our complexions more seriously. We actually wash our faces with soap and water, and 'Lady Veronica' says here that that's an absolutely suicidal practice for delicate skins. She gives all kinds of recipes for what one should do. I wish I could have a few lessons in face massage. I wonder how hard one ought to rub? And why a downward movement all the time?" (Beatrice was stroking her cheeks contemplatively as she spoke.) "Why mayn't you rub upwards?"

"The Princess recommends gentle pinching," said Mollie Hill, who was studying the columns of a rival paper, "and then an application of Mrs. Courtenay's lavender cream. We ought to be careful not to get freckled or sunburnt. 'Lady Marjorie' gives some splendid prescriptions against both. I wonder how the papers always get the aristocracy to write their Beauty Hints? I shouldn't have thought they'd have condescended to reveal their secrets!"

"My good girl! Don't flatter yourself that either 'Lady Veronica' or 'Lady Marjorie' is a member of the aristocracy," chuckled Bessie Kirk. "They're probably most plebeian and dowdy-looking individuals living in Bloomsbury boarding-houses, with pasty complexions and freckled noses, and they get a percentage on the preparations they recommend. If you notice, they always tell you to use Mrs. Somebody's pomade or face cream, and it's generally very expensive."

"Oh, but this one's home-made!" declared Beatrice. "Look here! It says: 'Take an ounce of spermaceti, and melt it in a pan with a teacupful of rose water. When thoroughly mixed, add an ounce of Vodax, which may be obtained from any chemist, stir until quite cold, then put into pots.' I'm sure that sounds simple enough, in all conscience."

Angela Brazil

"What about the Vodax, though? If you went to the chemist's you'd find it is a patent preparation, and very expensive, and it would just knock the bottom out of the 'home-made' theory of the recipe."

"There must be something in all these hints, though," said Mollie plaintively, "or the paper wouldn't publish them every week."

"Well, perhaps there is, to a certain extent, but just think of the time it would take to carry them out, to say nothing of the expense of cosmetics. Here, give me the book a sec, and a piece of pencil. I want to make a calculation. Now, if you really follow 'Lady Marjorie's' advice, your day will run something like this. It's a kind of beauty time-table:

```
Face Massage, Morning........................ 10 minutes
    "       "      Evening........................... 10  "
Hair Drill, Morning........................... 15  "
    "       "      Evening........................... 15  "
Application of cloths wrung out in hot water to face daily 30  "
Breathing Exercises............................ 15  "
Physical        "   ...................................... 15  "
Manicure.............................................5   "
Oatmeal applications...........................5   "
-------------------------------------------------------------------
Total  ................................................ 2 hours.
```

"Now, if you're going to put in two hours every day at your toilet, it seems to me that you won't have much time left for games, unless you can get your prep. excused on the ground that you're studying beauty culture. I'd like to see Bunty's face if you asked her!"

"Don't be piggish!" said Mollie. "One has no need to cultivate a tough skin, just because one's fond of cricket and hockey. I hate to see girls with hard red cheeks and freckles."

It was certainly not possible to obtain Mrs. Courtenay's

lavender cream or any other toilet specialties at the Camp. Beatrice and Mollie, however, impressed with the necessity of preserving their complexions, commandeered some of the buttermilk which was sent daily from the farm, and dabbed it plentifully over their faces before retiring to bed, following the application with massage to the best of their ability. They were emulated in these toilet rites by Agatha James, Mary Payne and Olave Parry, who also studied the beauty hints columns, and liked to try experiments. One day Agatha found an entirely new suggestion in a copy of "The Ladies' Portfolio." A correspondent wrote strongly advocating common salt as a hair tonic. It was to be rubbed in at night, and brushed out again in the morning.

Apparently nothing could be more simple. Beatrice, being on kitchen duty, had access to the salt-box. She purloined a good breakfastcupful, and divided the spoils with her four confederates. They all rubbed the salt carefully into the roots of their hair. Next morning, however, when they essayed to brush it out again, it obstinately refused to budge, and remained hard and gritty among their tresses. They were very much concerned. What was to be done? The only obvious remedy was to wash their hair. Now the one drawback of the Camp was its shortage of water. The daily supply had to be carried in buckets from the farm, and as, owing to the warm dry weather, the well was getting low, their allowance at present was rather small, and had to be carefully husbanded. The amount doled out for washing purposes certainly was quite inadequate for the due rinsing of five plentiful heads of hair.

"I suppose we shall just have to grin and bear it till we can get home and can mermaid properly in a bath!" sighed Mary.

"Oh, I can't! I'm going to wash mine somehow. Look here, suppose we sneak off quietly this afternoon, and go on a water hunt?"

"There isn't a stream or a pond anywhere near."

"We haven't tried the wood!"

"Well, we're not allowed there, of course."

"I don't see why we shouldn't go. The young pheasants must be all hatched, and running about by this time, so what harm could we do? Besides which, nobody's troubling about preserving game during the war. They're shooting Germans instead of birds this year."

"Very likely the gamekeeper has enlisted," suggested Beatrice, "in which case there'd be no one to stop us."

Now the strict law of the Camp confined the girls to the pasture, but as it was the last week of the quarantine, they were beginning to grow a little slack about rules. The five victims of the salt cure waited until Miss Huntley and Nurse Robinson were enjoying their afternoon siesta; then, without waiting for any permission, they climbed the fence into the lane, found a thin place in the hedge, and scrambled into the wood. It was a thrillingly exciting experience. Rather scratched and panting, they surveyed the prospect. Trees were everywhere, with a thick undergrowth of bramble and bracken. Apparently there was no path at all.

"I suppose we shall just have to wander about till we see a pond!" remarked Agatha.

"I believe some people can find water with a forked hazel twig," said Olave. "They hold it loosely in their hands, and it jerks when the water's near. I wish I knew how to do it!"

"Oh, water-finders are occult people," laughed Beatrice, "the sort that see spooks and do table-turning, you know. Besides, they find underground water, and tell where wells ought to be dug. We want a pond which any one can see with the naked eye, without being endowed with psychic powers. My natural reason tells me to go down hill, and perhaps we'll strike it in a hollow."

The girls rambled on, thoroughly enjoying the coolness of the shade and the beauty of the wood. As Beatrice had prophesied, when they reached the foot of the incline they came across quite a good-sized pool, with reeds and iris growing on its banks. They rejoiced exceedingly.

Now it is one thing to wash one's hair in a bath or a basin, but quite another to perform that operation in a pond with shallow muddy edges. The girls took off their shoes and stockings, tucked up their skirts and waded into the middle, where they made gallant efforts at dipping and rinsing their heads, and contrived to get uncommonly wet in the process. They wrung out their dripping tresses, mopped them with handkerchiefs (for nobody had dared to take a towel), and spread them out over their shoulders to dry. There was an open glade close by, where they could squat in the sunshine, and let the breeze help the process. Mary had had the forethought to put a comb in her pocket and she lent it round in turns. They were sitting in a row, like five mermaids, extremely complacent and satisfied with themselves, when footsteps suddenly crashed through the wood, and a middle-aged man approached them. For once Beatrice's calculations were wrong. The gamekeeper had not yet enlisted. No doubt he would have been far better employed in the trenches some-where in France, but here he was, still in England, and looking extremely surly and truculent.

"You've no business to be in this wood," he began. "Can't you read the trespass notices? There's plenty of them about. What do you mean by coming in here, disturbing the pheasants?"

"We aren't doing any harm!" protested Olave.

"That's neither here nor there. You've no business here, and you know it! Are you from that camp up the hill?"

"Yes."

"Then take yourselves off at once - spreading small-pox!"

"We've none of us had small-pox!" returned Beatrice indignantly. "We've told you we weren't doing any harm. Still, if this will make things right -" and she slipped half-a-crown into his hand.

The gamekeeper's expression changed considerably, and his tone instantly became more respectful.

"Well, young ladies, I have to do my duty, and of course you understand the pheasants mustn't be disturbed anyhow. Perhaps you won't mind going back to the Camp now. I'll show you a path that will take you into the lane."

He led the way, and the girls followed in subdued silence, feeling rather crestfallen. Mollie was yearning to tell him that he ought to be doing his duty by his country instead of by the pheasants. If at that moment she could have found a white feather, I believe she would have presented it to him. The path ended in a small gate which he unlocked. He ushered them solemnly into the lane, pointed out a trespass notice that was nailed conspicuously on to a tree, and then retired into the fastnesses of the wood. The girls decided that, unless actually compelled, they would not divulge where they had been.

"It was a bit of hard luck to be caught!" giggled Olave. "Didn't you feel queer when he came up?"

"I thought he was a beast, and didn't deserve propitiating with a tip!" declared Agatha.

"But we washed our hair!" rejoiced Mary, plaiting her long dark pigtail.

CHAPTER XII

CAPTAIN WINONA

To the entire satisfaction of themselves, their relations, and Dr. Barnes, the girls passed safely through their period of quarantine, and were certified as fit once more to take their places among the rest of the world. They left the Camp almost with regret. They had been such a jolly, merry party, and had enjoyed such high jinks there, that they felt their departure closed a pleasant episode. They were going straight home to holidays, however, which was a very different matter from returning to work. The remainder of July and the month of August passed very swiftly to Winona. She missed Percy, who was in training with his regiment, but since the advent of their new governess, Letty and Mamie had grown more sensible, and proved quite pleasant companions. Letty especially seemed suddenly to have awakened, so far as her intellectual capacities were concerned. She had begun to devour Scott and Dickens, took a keen interest in nature study, and tried - sometimes with rather comical effect - to be extremely superior and grown-up.

"She's far cleverer really than I am," thought Winona. "Pity she's not at the Seaton High! She'd be the star of her form directly. I wish she could get a scholarship some day."

With her school experience in coaching juniors, Winona was able to give her family some drilling in the matter of cricket, though she did not find that younger brothers and sisters proved such docile pupils as the members of III.a. and III.b. It was the usual case of "a prophet is not without honor, save in his own country," and while to High School juniors she preserved the authority and dignity of a senior, to Letty, Mamie, Ernie, Godfrey, and Dorrie she was "only Winona." She practiced tennis with the Vicarage girls, and was surprised to find how much her play had improved. Last summer they had nearly always beaten her, now it was she who scored the victories.

"I've learnt how to play games at 'The High,' even if my report was only moderate," she said to herself.

To make up for the long holiday caused by the small-pox scare, school was to commence at the beginning of September. Aunt Harriet, who had not been well, and was taking a rest in Scotland, wrote that her house in Abbey Close was shut up for the present, but that she was making other arrangements for her great-niece until her return. This term a hostel was to be opened in connection with the High School, and Winona was to be a boarder there for a few weeks. She was uncertain whether she liked the prospect or not, but she nevertheless left home in good spirits.

The hostel was under the superintendence of Miss Kelly. It was prettily furnished, and looked bright and pleasant. The girls had a common sitting-room, where they could read, write, paint or play games, and the bedrooms were divided into cubicles. So far there were only ten boarders, though there was accommodation for eighteen, but no doubt the numbers would be increased when the venture became better known.

The school seemed very strange without the familiar figures of Margaret Howell, Kirsty Paterson, Patricia Marshall and the other prefects. All of the Sixth had left except Linda Fletcher and Dorrie Pollock, and the members of V.a. were now promoted to the top form. Linda Fletcher was head of the school, the new prefects being Hilda Langley, Agatha James, Bessie Kirk, Grace Olliver, Evelyn Richards and Garnet

Emerson. Linda, with her past year's experience, made an extremely suitable "Head." She understood thoroughly what ought to be done, and at once called a mass meeting of the whole school in the gymnasium. Everybody clapped as Linda stood up on the platform to open the proceedings. She had been a favorite as a prefect, so she was welcomed in her new capacity of "General."

"Girls!" she began. "I felt it was better to lose no time in calling this meeting to settle the affairs of the coming school year. I am in a difficult position, because I have to follow such an extremely able and efficient 'Head.' I'm afraid I can't hope to rival Margaret Howell (cries of "Yes! Yes!" and "You'll do!" from the audience), but at least I shall try to do my duty. During the past year we may fairly consider that the 'Seaton High' made enormous strides. Owing to the exertions of our former 'Head' and prefects a most excellent foundation has been laid. The Dramatic Society, the Debating Club, the Literary Association, the Photographic Union and the Natural History League all accomplished very satisfactory work, and may be considered in a most flourishing condition. Perhaps, though, our greatest improvement is in the direction of games. This may not appear on the surface, for though we won five hockey matches, it was impossible, for reasons well known to you, to have fixtures for hockey and tennis. We feel, nevertheless, that in spite of our inability to test our skill against that of other schools we are conscious of the enormous all-round improvement that has taken place in our play. It was Kirsty Paterson's policy to train recruits for the games so that every girl in the school might be a possible champion. How well she succeeded I hope our next season's matches may testify. Let us all work together for the good of the school, and try to establish the reputation of the 'Seaton High.' I need not remind you that everything in the coming year will depend upon the energy and efficiency of the Games Captain. As soon as I knew that I was 'Head,' I wrote to Kirsty, who is staying in Cornwall, and asked for her opinion upon this most important point. I want to read you an extract from her reply, which I received this morning. She says:

"'You ask me who is to be the new Games Captain. Well, of course it is a delicate matter to nominate my own successor, but from my knowledge of everybody's capacities I should most decidedly suggest Winona Woodward. She is a good all-round player herself, and has a particular aptitude for organization, which should prove invaluable. She thoroughly appreciates the advantage of having reserves to fall back upon, and is most keen on keeping up the standard. I do hope the dear old "High" will have a splendid year. I shall be frantic to hear how you get on. Send me a p.c. with the result of the meeting.'

"Well," continued Linda, "you've heard Kirsty's opinion. It coincides entirely with mine. Will some one kindly propose that Winona Woodward shall be elected Games Captain?"

"I have much pleasure in making the proposal," said Bessie Kirk, standing up promptly.

"And I have much pleasure in seconding it," murmured Grace Olliver.

"Will all who are in favor kindly hold up their hands? Carried unanimously! I'm extremely glad, as I'm sure Winona is 'the right man for the job,' and worthy to carry on Kirsty's traditions. I vote we give her three cheers!"

Winona flushed crimson as the hip-hip-hoorays rang forth. She had never expected such a complete walk-over. She had known that her name was to be submitted for the captaincy, but she had thought that Bessie Kirk and Marjorie Kemp held equal chances, and that the voting would probably be fairly evenly divided. That Kirsty should have written to nominate her was an immense gratification. Kirsty's praise at the time had been scant, and Winona had no idea that her former chief held her in such esteem. To Winona the occasion seemed the triumph of her life. She would rather be Games Captain than have any other honor that could possibly be offered to her. Glorious visions of successful matches, of shields or cups won, and a county reputation for the school swam before her eyes. And she - Winona Woodward - was to have the privilege of leading and directing all this! It was indeed a thrilling prospect. Her thoughts went back to the symposium of a year ago, when as a new and unknown girl, she had listened to Margaret Howell's inspiring speech. How unlikely it had seemed then that she would ever have a hand in making school history, but how her spirit had been stirred, and how she had longed to do her part! It was something to have realized her pet ambition.

"It was most awfully good of you to propose me," she said to Bessie Kirk afterwards. "You'd a splendid chance yourself."

"Not I!" returned Bessie lightly. "Kirsty's letter settled the whole business. I shouldn't have made nearly as good a Captain as you. I don't care to bother with the kids, and I'd hate all the business part of it, making the fixtures and that sort of thing, you know. You'll be A1, and we'll all play up no end. I believe we dare venture a fixture with Grant Park this season."

Winona fully realized the responsibilities of her important position, and began at once to pick up the threads of her new duties. She took possession of the Games Register, with its records of past matches, and began to make plans for hockey fixtures. The term had begun so early that the other schools in the county had not yet re-opened; that, however, was really an advantage, as it gave her more time for consideration. At present the September weather was hot as summer, and tennis and cricket were still in full swing. In order to spur on enthusiasm Winona organized a school tennis tournament. The result was highly satisfactory. Several new and unsuspected stars swam into view, and she determined to keep her eye upon them as possible champions for next summer.

"You never know what a girl's capable of till you try her!" she confided to Garnet. "Who would ever have thought that that stupid-looking little Emily Cooper could beat Ethel March? I was simply astounded. I've my plans for Emily, I can tell you!

And I believe Bertha March is going to be a second Annie Hardy. She serves in exactly the same way. Oh, I've hopes for next summer. Brilliant, glorious hopes."

The school took every opportunity of using the fine weather while it lasted. The Photographic Union organized an outing to Linworth, a picturesque town six miles away, where an old castle, an Elizabethan mansion, a river and many quaint streets made subjects for their cameras, and promised to provide materials for an exhibition later on, when films were developed and prints taken. The Natural History League had another delightful ramble under Miss Lever's leadership, and secured additional specimens for the museum. On this occasion Winona and Garnet started in better time for the station, and did not get into the wrong train, as they had done on the expedition to Monkend Woods.

"Dollikins," as Miss Lever was affectionately nicknamed, was as great a favorite as ever among the girls. Owing to changes on the staff, she now had charge of IV.a. and taught mathematics throughout the junior forms, so that the seniors saw little of her in school hours. On a ramble she was as jolly as one of themselves.

The Sixth had a new mistress, Miss Goodson, who had only joined the staff this term. The form was rather uncertain whether to like her or not. It was rumored that she had been engaged specially to coach them for the matriculation. So far the High School had been laying foundations, and had not sent in any candidates for public examinations. This year, however, having a certain amount of promising material in the Sixth, Miss Bishop had decided that the time was ripe for trying to win the educational laurels towards which their training had been directed. Miss Goodson came from a High School in the north, and brought with her a reputation for successful coaching. She was well up in all her subjects, but she was a cold and not very inspiring person. She was apt to concentrate her energies on the clever members of her form, and leave the less brilliant to stumble along as best they could.

Winona, who certainly belonged to the second category, did not like Miss Goodson, while Garnet was strongly in her favor.

In her new capacity of prefect, Garnet proved a success. She was as enthusiastic over the "bookish" side of the school as Winona over the athletic department. She was President of the Literary Association, a member of the Debating Club Committee, and head librarian. The school library had grown and prospered exceedingly since its installation by Margaret Howell. It now numbered nearly five hundred volumes, and its shelves almost filled the Prefects' Room. Garnet managed it systematically. She had special hours at which books were issued, and assistants whose business it was to be on duty at the specified times.

Among other improvements in the school welcomed by the girls was the advent of a fresh drilling mistress, and some new apparatus for gymnastics. Under Miss Barbour, "Gym" became highly popular, and it was felt that an athletic display would probably be held at Christmas. This was something to work for, and every one seemed much keener than formerly. Winona was naturally an enthusiast, and tried to keep others up to the mark. She had once seen an "Assault-at-Arms" at Percy's college, and the memory of it made her long for the Seaton High School to have a similar opportunity of showing its prowess. She and a select circle of friends practiced whenever possible. Altogether among the various athletic activities of the school, Captain Winona promised herself a very enjoyable year in the Sixth Form.

CHAPTER XIII

THE HOSTEL

Aunt Harriet had intended to return home towards the end of September, but her health continued so unsatisfactory that her doctor ordered her to Harrogate to drink the waters, and advised a long period of rest and change before again taking up the many occupations with which she busied herself in Seaton. Miss Beach was a restive patient, and Dr. Sidwell knew that if he once allowed her to be within reach of committees, she would plunge herself into work, while to keep away from the scenes of her former activity was her only chance of recovery.

The house in Abbey Close was still shut up, and Winona for the present term was established at the Hostel. On the whole she liked it. She missed certain things, particularly her own bedroom, and the quiet dining-room where she had been accustomed to prepare her lessons, but life in a community had its compensations. It was a nuisance to have to sleep in the same dormitory with Betty Carlisle, who snored offensively, but, on the other hand, Winona's cubicle was next to the window, with the little balcony that overlooked the park, and every morning she could watch an aeroplane hovering and flitting like a beautiful dragon-fly over the city. Seaton possessed a Government aircraft factory, and each finished machine had to be carefully tested. All the girls in the school were extremely interested in the exploits of Lieutenant Mainwaring, a member of the Flying Corps, who might constantly be seen practicing. He was a cousin of Elsie Mainwaring, a

Fifth Form girl. Elsie recorded his doings with immense pride, and provided up-to-date information of his whereabouts. He was a very daring young fellow, and was reported to have looped the loop. Winona had never witnessed the performance of this feat, so she looked out eagerly each day, hoping she might have the luck to see him do it. When the biplane came swooping over the park, she would wave her handkerchief to it from the balcony by way of encouragement. She was immensely patriotic, and she considered that our airmen deserved praise almost beyond any other branch of our forces. She often wished Percy were in the Flying Squadron. She cut out all the pictures of aeroplanes from the Seaton *Graphic*, and pinned them up in her cubicle. There was a portrait of Lieutenant Mainwaring among the number, and this she placed on her dressing-table, side by side with Percy's photograph. According to Elsie it was a very bad likeness, but as Winona had not seen the original, except at a distance, she had no means of judging. Curiosity led her to borrow a pair of field-glasses from Garnet. She was standing one morning on the balcony when the aeroplane came in sight, and hovered quite low down over the park, exactly opposite the hostel windows. Through her glasses Winona could plainly see the occupant. The impulse to smile and wave was irresistible. To her immense surprise the signal was returned. In frantic excitement she waved again, and shouted "Hooray!"

"What are you doing, Winona Woodward?" snapped a voice behind her, and turning guiltily, she found herself face to face with Miss Kelly.

"I - I was only looking at the aeroplane," stammered Winona.

"Come in at once! You know perfectly well that this sort of thing is not allowed. I am very much surprised and disgusted. If I find you signaling to gentlemen again from this balcony, I shall change your dormitory. Whose field-glasses are those?"

"Garnet Emerson's," said Winona sulkily.

"Then you must give them back to Garnet this morning. Remember, that such unladylike conduct must never happen again at the hostel."

Winona considered herself very much aggrieved. She had waved on the spur of the moment, and to have her innocent and impulsive act construed into "signaling to gentlemen," and reproved as "unladylike conduct," was highly aggravating. Miss Kelly was a disciplinarian, and of a very suspicious temperament. Her idea of duty was the French one of "surveillance." She never trusted the girls, or put them upon their honor; her mode of procedure was to keep an eye upon them, and to pop in suddenly and surprise them. They resented this attitude extremely.

"Miss Kelly always gives us credit for going to do the very worst!" grumbled Betty Carlisle.

"She puts ideas into our heads!" declared Doris Hooper indignantly.

The gist of the trouble was this: the girls at the hostel expected to have as much liberty as if they were in their own homes, while Miss Kelly, who had formerly been a mistress at St. Chad's, wished to enforce strict boarding-school rules. It was much more difficult to do this because the hostel only formed part of a large day school; the general atmosphere of the place was more free than at a college where all alike are boarders, and the girls naturally were infected by the prevailing spirit. A constant source of annoyance was the rule that they must report themselves in the hostel at 4.15. It was the fashion to linger after school, and chat in the "gym" or in the playground. It was a delightful little time, when everybody could meet every one else, and discuss school news and matches and guilds and other interesting topics. To be obliged, for no particular reason, to cut short their conversations and race back to the hostel was annoying. The boarders evaded the rule as far as possible, but Miss Kelly kept a roll-call, and they knew that their absences would be duly reported to Miss Bishop.

To Winona, in especial, many of the rules were extremely irksome. At more than sixteen and a half, she felt it ridiculous to be obliged to ask permission to go out and buy a lead pencil at the stationer's. "It's like living in a convent!" she fumed.

Another bone of contention was her preparation. She had been so accustomed to work in a room by herself at Abbey Close that she found the presence of others highly distracting. Though silence was enforced, the girls fluttered the leaves of their books, scratched with their pens, or even murmured dates under their breath, all of which sounds were most irritating. Winona begged to be allowed to take her books to her cubicle, but Miss Kelly would not hear of it.

"I cannot make an exception for one," she replied, "and it would be impossible to allow girls to work as they liked in the dormitories. There would be more talking than preparation! You'll stay here with the others, and I can see for myself what you're doing."

The hint that Miss Kelly suspected her of some ulterior motive for wishing to study upstairs enraged Winona, but she was obliged to submit, and to sit, close under the mistress' eye, at the long table, in company with her fellow-boarders. Her work suffered in consequence, and Miss Goodson's sarcasms descended on her head. Miss Goodson was not so patient a teacher as Miss Huntley, and Winona tried her temper at times. Winona was subject to curious fits of stupidity. Her brains were like a clock with a broken cog. Sometimes they would work easily, and on other days she seemed quite unable to grasp the most obvious problems. A lively imagination may be a very delightful possession, and of use in the writing of history and literature exercises, but it cannot supply the place of solid facts, nor is it of the least aid in mathematics, so Winona's form record was not high.

The hockey season would commence at the beginning of October, but during September, while the weather was still warm, the girls continued to play cricket on Wednesdays. The school was fortunate enough to possess large playing fields; these adjoined the public park, in itself a big area, so that quite a fine open space lay below the buildings. One afternoon, just as Winona was having her innings, Elsie Mainwaring uttered a cry, and pointed overhead. Far up in the clouds was the aeroplane, and it was gracefully looping the loop.

"It's Harry! He's showing off for our benefit!" squealed Elsie excitedly. "I told him we should be playing cricket to-day. Oh! didn't he do it cleverly? He went just straight head over heels in the air! Let's wave to him, and perhaps he'll come down a little."

Handkerchiefs fluttered out so briskly that the field resembled a washing day. Miss Barbour was signaling as vigorously as the rest. Evidently Lieutenant Mainwaring took the display for an invitation, the biplane descended like a hawk, and to every one's immense gratification alighted on the school ground. To see a real live airman at such close quarters was not an ordinary experience. Elsie promptly introduced her cousin to Miss Barbour and begged that they might all inspect the machine. Lieutenant Mainwaring good-naturedly explained the various parts; perhaps he rather enjoyed a visit to a Ladies' School! He did not stay long, however, but after a few minutes started his engine and went soaring up again into the blue of the sky, and wheeling over the towers of the old Minster was soon lost to sight behind some clouds.

"It must be glorious to fly!" sighed Winona.

In spite of Miss Kelly's injunctions she could not help looking out of her window every morning for the aeroplane, and giving a surreptitious wave. She told herself that she was only acting patriotically in cheering on our aerial defenses. The back of the hostel opened into the school playground, and one day Winona, taking a run there for exercise before breakfast, heard the familiar whirring, and looking up, beheld the flying-machine poised just overhead. She heard a shout from the occupant, and something dropped into the playground. She ran to pick it up. It was a packet of chocolates! She tried to wave thanks, but the biplane had moved on, and was now far over the town, Lieutenant Mainwaring no doubt having enjoyed his little joke of innocent bomb-dropping.

Now most unfortunately for Winona, Miss Kelly's bedroom window overlooked the playground, and she had been a witness of the whole incident. She came out now in extreme wrath, confiscated the chocolates, and scolded Winona sharply.

"But it's not my fault! I'd no idea he was going to drop anything!" protested Winona indignantly.

"After what has happened before, I can only draw my own conclusions," returned the mistress icily. "You will change to Number 3 dormitory to-day."

"But, Miss Kelly -"

"Don't argue! I warned you that I should move you if I found any more signaling going on. Your aunt will have to hear about this!"

When Winona returned to the hostel that afternoon, and went upstairs, she found that all her possessions had been cleared out of Number 2 dormitory, and placed in Number 3, which being at the side of the house had no view except the school buildings. The contents of her drawers had been transferred intact; her brushes, books and home photos were placed on her new dressing-table, but all the pictures of aeroplanes and the portrait of Lieutenant Mainwaring, which she had cut out of the Seaton *Graphic*, had disappeared. Winona sat down on the bed and laughed. She was very much annoyed, but the humor of the situation appealed to her.

"It's too idiotic of Miss Kelly! Does she think I'm going to elope in an aeroplane? I never heard of anything so silly in my life! She may tell Aunt Harriet if she pleases. I don't care! Why,

I don't suppose Lieutenant Mainwaring knows me from any other girl in the school. He just dropped those chocs. on spec. It was a shame I wasn't allowed to eat them!"

Miss Kelly, very keen on upholding discipline in her new hostel, considered that she had successfully squashed an incipient flirtation, and kept a stern eye on all the elder girls, and most particularly on Winona, for fear some repetition of the offense might occur. The boarders were justly indignant.

"Too bad!" was the general verdict. "Winona's not a scrap that sort of girl really, if Miss Kelly only knew. It's absurd to make such a fuss."

Out of sheer bravado and love of mischief, the remaining occupants of Number 2 dormitory waved not only hand-kerchiefs but towels from the balcony when they heard the whirring of the aeroplane overhead, enjoying the exciting sensation that any moment they might be pounced upon by Miss Kelly. No doubt in time they would have been discovered in the act, but at the end of three days Lieutenant Mainwaring was sent to the front, and his successor, not having a cousin at the Seaton High School, took no interest in school girls, and flew over the city oblivious of everything except his engines.

"I don't suppose he'd notice if we waved a sheet!" said Betty Carlisle disappointedly.

"The police might though, and they'd think you were signaling to Germans," replied Doris Hooper. "Come in, Bet, it's no use! Girl alive, quick! I hear the dragon's fairy footsteps in the passage. Do you want to get your head bitten off?"

In spite of occasional hostilities with Miss Kelly, Winona managed to have a good deal of fun at the hostel. The other girls were jolly, and in the evenings, when preparation was finished, they would play games together in their sitting-room. There were high jinks in the dormitories, and small excitements over little happenings, which, however trivial they might be, provided considerable entertainment to the participants. Only one really stormy incident occurred during Winona's term at the hostel, and that had nothing to do with Miss Kelly.

One Saturday morning, when Winona, Betty and Doris were in the town shopping, they happened to meet Clarice Nixon, who stopped to chat, and ask for school news.

"I feel fearfully out of things now I've left," said Clarice. "It'll be a stale winter without hockey."

"Why don't you join a Club?" suggested Winona.

"Shouldn't care to! It would be no fun to play with a team I don't know. The Seaton Ladies' Club is the only decent one, and I hear they're so cliquey. I wish we could get up an Old Girls' Hockey Club!"

"Why, that would be simply glorious! What a splendiferous idea! Oh, do let us try! Then we could have a Past *versus* Present match. Oh! wouldn't it be precious?"

"Have you settled up your fixtures?"

"Very nearly."

"Then we ought to get this thing in hand at once. You're Games Captain, so you ought to organize it. Write round to-day to all the old girls you know, and ask them to come to a meeting on Monday."

"Isn't that rather soon?" said Betty.

"Not a bit. No time must be wasted, if the club's to be a going concern for this season. Don't let the grass grow under your feet, is my advice."

Winona was naturally impulsive. The idea appealed to her so immensely, that she straightway bought a packet of postcards and a number of halfpenny stamps, and sent out her invitations. As she was bound to report herself in the hostel at 4.15, she decided to call the meeting there at 4.20. It could be held in the sitting-room, and there would be plenty of time to discuss matters before five o'clock tea. She wrote to Margaret Howell, Kirsty Paterson, and all the former members of the Sixth, and was already exulting over the success which she hoped would accrue. She was sure every one in the school would like the notion when they heard about it.

On Monday morning when she walked into her form room, she noticed several of the prefects talking together. They looked at her significantly as she entered, and Evelyn Richards made a movement as if about to speak. Grace Olliver, how-ever, laid her hand on Evelyn's arm, and pointed to the clock, as if deferring the matter. At eleven "break," as the girls filed out of the room, Agatha James laid a paper on Winona's desk. It bore the words:

"Kindly report yourself at once in the prefects' room."

Rather mystified, Winona obeyed the summons. She found the prefects assembled in their den, looking dignified and perturbed.

"Winona Woodward," began Linda Fletcher, "are you responsible for this post-card?" showing one of the invitations which had been written on Saturday. "Beatrice Howell brought it to me first thing this morning, by Margaret's advice. Margaret couldn't understand why you had sent it to her."

"I explained on the card," replied Winona eagerly. "It was to try to get up an Old Girls' Hockey Club!"

"And who gave you authority to call such a meeting?" asked Linda icily.

"Why, I thought as Games Captain -" began Winona, then she stopped, for the faces of the prefects expressed a righteous wrath that staggered her.

"It was a most unwarrantable liberty!" continued the head girl. "As Games Captain you are responsible for the school play and for the fixtures, but you're certainly not to take upon yourself a matter of this kind. Why, you're not even a prefect! And no prefect would have dreamed of calling such a meeting on her own account without consulting her colleagues."

"I - thought - there wasn't time - to ask," stammered Winona, overcome with confusion.

"As a matter of fact the suggestion had already been placed before the prefects, and it was proposed to form an Old Girls' Guild, which would include several branches, a Hockey Club being among the number. An initial committee meeting is to be held next Thursday. Margaret Howell was perfectly well aware of this, and could not understand why you should have stepped in and called a meeting at the hostel, thus forestalling our arrangements."

"It's the most abominable cheek I ever heard of!" burst out Agatha James.

"What were you dreaming of?" demanded Grace Olliver.

Poor Winona! She suddenly saw her innocent, impulsive act in the light in which it must appear to the prefects. It had never struck her that she was exceeding her authority, and that she ought to have referred the matter to the head of the school. The urgency of getting the club started, so as to enter a Past *v.* Present in her list of fixtures, had been her uppermost thought. She had indeed made a most terrible blunder. The feeling against her was evidently one of general censure. Even Garnet looked grave, and Bessie Kirk was bridling. Linda's manner was coldly official. The stateliness of her speech was more cutting than Agatha's explosive wrath. Winona collapsed utterly, and groveled.

"I'm most fearfully sorry!" she apologized. "Indeed I'd never have done it if I'd thought about it. I was an utter idiot! I really don't know what possessed me! I just sent off those cards in a hurry. What shall I do? There isn't time to write back to everybody!"

"I think I can send messages to most of the girls, and if any turn up at the hostel this afternoon they must be told." Linda's tone was slightly mollified. "I hardly need impress upon you the necessity in future of referring everything to headquarters. No school can be run on the basis of individual enterprise."

Duly chastened, Winona left the prefects' room. She had the further annoyance in the afternoon of explaining the situation to several comers who turned up in answer to her invitation. Notwithstanding this preliminary disturbance, the Old Girls' Guild was started with thirty-five members on the roll. A Hockey Club and a Dramatic Society were formed, both of which promised to have a flourishing existence, and Winona had the satisfaction of fixing a Past *v.* Present match for the following March. The prefects were magnanimous enough to bear her no ill-will, so on the whole she came out of a very unpleasant dilemma much better than she expected.

CHAPTER XIV

THE HOCKEY SEASON

When the hockey season commenced, Winona got to business. She was wildly anxious to prove an effective Games Captain, and win credit for the school. It would be no easy matter to follow so excellent a predecessor as Kirsty Paterson, but she determined to keep Kirsty's ideals well in mind, and try to live up to them. One change, which Kirsty had suggested, Winona at once carried out. The hockey badge was altered. The new one had the initials S.H.S. embroidered in the school colors on plain dark blue shields, and looked very imposing on the tunics. There was another point upon which Winona was resolved to effect a reform. The field was not in a thoroughly satisfactory condition, and certainly needed attention. The prefects had put the matter before Miss Bishop, who referred it to the Governors. Those august personages, mindful of war economies, decided that for the present it would do well enough, and would not vote the spending of any money upon its improvement. The bad news was received with indignation throughout the school.

"It's too stingy for anything! How can we possibly have decent practice on such a rough old place? I'd like to make them come and try it for themselves, the mean wretches!" protested Bessie Kirk.

Winona laughed. A vision of the Governors wildly brandishing hockey sticks flashed across her imagination. She seized her

Angela Brazil

note-book and drew a fancy portrait of the delicious scene: old Councillor Thomson, very wheezy and fat, running furiously; bald-headed Mr. Crabbe performing wonderful acrobatic feats; a worthy J.P. engaged in a tussle with the Town Clerk; and various other of the City Fathers in interesting and exciting attitudes. The masterpiece was passed round for general admiration. The girls sniggered.

"Wish we could show it to them!" said Margaret Kemp. "Perhaps it might make them realize their responsibilities. It's too sickening of them to grudge keeping the field in order!"

"Look here, it's no use complaining!" said Winona. "Of course it relieves one's feelings, but it doesn't make any difference to the field. I've got a plan to propose. Let us ask Miss Bishop how much it would cost to hire somebody to do the rolling, and offer to pay for it ourselves. We could get up a Hockey Concert in aid of it."

"What a frolicsome notion! I'm your man!"

"Wouldn't it be setting a bad precedent?" objected Marjorie Kemp. "Suppose the Governors stop having the tennis courts cut, and say we may do it ourselves?"

"We'd put that to Miss Bishop first, and make it well understood."

"It would just make all the difference to the practices to have a roller at work, even once a week," urged Olave Parry. "Do ask about it, Win!"

Miss Bishop, on being appealed to, considered the suggestion favorably.

"Certainly there's no reason why you shouldn't improve the field, if you wish," she replied, adding with a smile: "I'll take care that the tennis courts don't suffer in consequence. It was a prudent thought to mention them. I expect when the war is over, the Governors may be persuaded to take the full expense of the playing field too. I'll get an estimate at once of what the rolling would cost."

Jones, the school janitor, who formerly kept the courts and cricket pitch in order, had gone to the war, and his place was occupied by a rheumatic old fellow who could do little more than carry coke and attend to the heating apparatus. When every able-bodied man seemed fighting or making munitions, it was difficult to find anybody to roll a hockey field, A volunteer was procured at last, however, who undertook the job at the rate of L1 per month, with an extra thirty shillings for putting the field in good order to begin with. Six or seven pounds, therefore, would cover the expenses of the season. Winona, mindful of the terrible offense she had given in connection with the Old Girls' Guild, very wisely took the matter to Linda Fletcher, who called a united meeting of Prefects and Games Committee to discuss the best way of raising the money.

"It will have to be done on a bigger scale than the symposium last year," said Hilda Langley. "If I remember rightly, that made exactly L2 13s. 7d., enough for a Form trophy, but not sufficient for this venture."

"We'd better issue tickets, and sell some of them to parents and friends," suggested Linda.

"How many will the hall hold?"

"Three hundred at a pinch, if the babes squash up tight."

"They won't mind doing that in a good cause."

"The Dramatic Society ought to take an innings, and provide at least half the program."

"They'll jump at the opportunity. I believe they have something quite prepared, and have been yearning for an audience."

"Then by all means let them have one."

"At sixpence a head," added practical Marjorie; "we ought easily to be able to sell sixpenny tickets."

Everybody took up the idea with enthusiasm. The difficulty was not so much to find helpers as to decide who was to have the honor of performing. There were many heart-burnings before the program was finally fixed. It was decided that a musical selection should be given first, followed by a piece by the Dramatic students. To cut these to reasonable limits needed all Linda's discretion, tact and firmness.

"You can't have an entertainment beginning at three, and going on till midnight," she urged, as the various desired items were submitted to her. "You'd have to hire ambulances to take your exhausted audience home! Very sorry, but we must keep some of the things for a future occasion."

Linda, being wise in her generation, and having an eye to the sale of tickets, insisted that the Lower School should take a share in the performance.

"Who wants to bother to hear the kids?" objected Grace Olliver, who, by the bye, was a member of the "Dramatic," and therefore not entirely disinterested.

"If we don't bother with the kids, they mayn't bother to come and bring friends, and we should look silly if we didn't sell all our tickets! Let them do their flag display, and sing their Empire song. That will content them and their mothers, and leaves quite time enough for other people."

Miss Bishop allowed a special Wednesday afternoon to be set aside for the entertainment; the tickets sold briskly, and expectation ran high. All concerned in the program kept their parts a dead secret, but items leaked out, and the wildest rumors were afloat. It was whispered that some of the Governors were to be present, and even that Miss Bishop would perform a sword dance, though not the most callow of juniors really consented to swallow such an astounding piece of information. The uncertainty as to what was in store, however, added largely to the pleasurable anticipation, and though the Dramatic Society rehearsed with locked door, and the keyhole carefully stopped up, juvenile spies, by hoisting one another up to the level of the windows, obtained brief and tantalizing peeps and spread news of gorgeosities in the way of costumes.

When the great afternoon arrived, the hall was crammed. The little girls were packed as tightly as sardines. A long line of them squatted on the floor in front of the first row, and others sat on the window sills, the latter positions having been scrambled for with enthusiasm.

Every one was at the tip-top of expectation. The concert opened with the inevitable piano solo which seems indispensable for the starting of any entertainment, and during the performance of which latecomers hurry to their seats, programs are sold, and the audience, with a tremendous amount of rustling and whispering, settles itself down to listen. This initiatory ceremony being over, more interesting items followed. The juveniles sang an Empire song, accompanied by a pretty flag drill; it was a taking tune, and as Linda had prophesied was immensely applauded by the visitors, who insisted on an encore. A violin solo came next, and was followed by a charming Russian dance given by two members of Form IV.a. Garnet played a piece on her mandoline, with piano accompaniment. She had suggested a duet for mandoline and guitar, but Winona had had no time to practice her instrument lately, and had begged to be excused. The fact was that Winona had been busy with a special item which she now brought out as a surprise to the school. She had composed some verses in praise of hockey, and set them to one of the tunes in the senior school song-book. The piece was sung by an eleven in full hockey costume, and they waved their hockey-sticks with appropriate actions to the music:

"When autumn returns, and the trees are all bare,

Our blue tunics are off to the field;
No team in excitement with ours can compare,
As our hockey-sticks wildly we wield.
For hockey's the game to play
When autumn has come to stay,
And this is the reason we love the cold season,
For hockey's the game to play.

"Hurrah for goalkeepers, for forwards and halves!
Hurrah for the clash of the sticks!
Hurrah for the rapture of scoring a goal!
(Who minds a few bruises or kicks?)
For hockey's the game to play,
When autumn has come to stay,
And this is the reason we love the cold season,
For hockey's the game to play.

"But a team that is set upon scoring its goal,
And winning a vict'ry or two,
Must see that its field it should carefully roll,
And that's what we're hoping to do!
Oh! hockey's the game to play,
When autumn has come to stay,
Yes, this is the reason we love the cold season,
When hockey's the game we play!

"Hurrah for Form trophies! Hurrah for our badge!
We'll make it an annual rule
To hold a 'Sports' Concert,' to wish all success
To the team of the Seaton High School!
Oh! hockey's the game to play,
And at Seaton we know the way!
Yes, this is the reason we love the cold season,
When hockey's the game we play!"

Winona's words would certainly not have passed muster as a literary composition, but their extreme appropriateness to the occasion, combined with the action of the hockey-sticks, completely brought down the house. The applause was thunderous, and the last verse was encored twice over. Undoubtedly it was the hit of the afternoon.

For the second part of the performance the Dramatic Society gave an amusing little play, and the concert wound up with a lusty rendering of certain patriotic songs.

Winona was highly gratified. Both artistically and financially the entertainment had proved a success. The committee would be well able to bear the expense of keeping the field in order. A gardener had been at work there, and already a marked improvement was noticeable. The Games Captain's enthusiasm was infectious. Under her leadership the girls became wonderfully keen. To Winona the thrill of struggle when a game seemed on the eve of being lost was one of the wildest excitements in life, and the joy when she struck the ball home straight and true the utmost triumph obtainable. During this autumn term she lived for hockey. The crowd of school girls, in thick boots and blue tunics, struggling and shouting in a somewhat muddy field might not be an altogether picturesque sight, but to the Captain it was Marathon and Waterloo combined. No colonel prided himself on a crack regiment more than Winona on her team. Sometimes, of course, a practice was off color; the day might be bleak or drizzly, or players might be penalized for "sticks," or grumblers might express their dissatisfaction audibly, but whatever went wrong, Winona emerged cheerful from the fray, remonstrated with "off-sides" and "sticks," and reminded growlers that it is unsporting to murmur. By Kirsty's advice she had sent out challenges to several good clubs in the neighborhood.

"While we were still in our callow infancy I should not have ventured," wrote Kirsty from Cornwall. "But one must begin some time to measure one's strength. After the work we did last season, I certainly think you might risk it. Nothing improves a team so much as playing plenty of matches; you see in time you get to know the strokes of everybody at the High, and you can calculate what others will do at certain turns of the game; it's far better for you to meet all sorts and conditions of opponents."

Winona had been afraid it was rather "cheek" to challenge the "West Rytonshire Club" or "Oatlands College," but she ascertained that both those august bodies had two teams, Number 1 and Number 2, and that while the first only met foes worthy of their steel (or rather sticks!) the second would graciously condescend to play a yet unknown High School. The match with Oatlands College was fixed for December 16th, and Winona looked forward to it with some anxiety. The last practice had not been altogether satisfactory. The day had been wretchedly cold, and everybody had been cross in consequence. The team, though proud of its fixture with so celebrated an opponent, was not very sure of itself.

"I hope to goodness Peggie'll play up!" groaned Marjorie Kemp. "The way she lost that last goal on Saturday was idiotic."

"She said she was cold!" commented Gladys Porter, with-ringly. "She wanted to change at half-time. She said her feet were solid ice, and her nose was blue, and it was no fun watching the whole of the game being played right away at the other end of the field."

"Most unsporting!" moralized Marjorie. "Besides, when she got her chance, she hit the air! It will be very humiliating if the Oatlands team walk over us!"

"Oh, don't be a Jeremiah! We're not beaten yet! If anybody can pull us through, our Captain will!"

"Winona's a jewel!" agreed Marjorie. "And yet the best captain in the world can't make up for an only moderately good team. I feel my own deficiencies!"

Practically the whole of the High School assembled as spectators on the great day of the match. Things were very different now from the old times when a mere handful collected to cheer the Seaton team. Mistresses and girls were alike keen, and most desirous of witnessing the combat. They followed the game breathlessly.

"Oatlands isn't worth a toss!" commented Garnet exultantly.

"Don't make too sure!" replied Linda, looking with apprehension as the red jerseys of their rivals massed round the ball.

A familiar figure dashed forward, a hockey stick struck, and the ball swept out to safety. Linda heaved a long sigh of relief.

"Winona is just A1," she murmured. "Hello! Good gracious! what's that idiot doing?"

For Ellinor Cooper, whose arm was the strongest in the school, wielding her hockey stick with all her force, had hit Winona across the shin.

Instantly there was a commotion. Winona, white with the agony of the blow, leaned hard against Bessie Kirk, and clenched her fists to avoid crying out.

"Are you hurt?"

"What's happened?"

"You've had a nasty knock!"

There was quite a crowd round Winona, and a chorus of sympathy.

"Put in a substitute!" urged Bessie. "You're not fit to go on!"

"No, no! I'm better now," panted their captain, with a wan little smile. "I'll manage, thanks! Yes, really! Please don't worry yourselves about me!"

The game recommenced and Winona, with a supreme effort,

continued to play. The pain was still acute, but she realized that on her presence or absence depended victory or defeat. Without her, the courage of the team would collapse. How she lived through the time she never knew.

Inspired by the heroic example of their captain, the girls were playing for all they were worth. The score, which had been against them, was now even. Time was almost up. Winona set her teeth. The ball seemed a kind of star which she was following - Following anyhow. As the French say, she "did her possible." The ball went spinning. Next minute she was leaning against a goal-post, trembling with the violence of her effort, while the High School hoorayed itself hoarse in the joy of the hard-won victory.

"I say, old girl, were you really hurt?" asked Bessie anxiously. "You're looking the color of chalk!"

"Never mind, it's over now! Yes, I am hurt. Give me your arm, and I'll go back to the hostel."

"You're an absolute Joan of Arc to-day!" purred Bessie.

Winona, with a barked shin and bad bruises, limped for more than a week, but she was the heroine of the school.

"I can't think how you ran, after that awful whack Ellinor Cooper gave you," sympathized Marjorie.

"It was easier to run then than after my leg grew stiff," laughed Winona. "I suppose it's the excitement that keeps one up. Don't make such a fuss, we've all had hard knocks in our time. Agnes Smith got a black eye last spring!"

As the result of her wounds in the hockey field Winona made friends with Miss Kelly. The latter was most prompt in applying lanoline and bandages, and proved so kind in bringing Winona her breakfast in bed, and making her rest on the sofa during preparation, that a funny little sort of intimacy sprang up between them.

"She's fussy on the surface, but nice when you know her," confided Winona to Garnet. "If I'd been staying at the hostel, I expect we should have got on capitally next term!"

Angela Brazil

CHAPTER XV

WINONA TURNS CHAUFFEUR

After the Christmas holidays Winona returned to Abbey Close. Miss Beach was installed once more in her own home, though under strict orders from the doctor not to over-exert herself. During her stay at Harrogate she had bought a small two-seater car, and had learnt to drive it. She kept it at a garage in the town, and used it almost every day. It was invaluable to her as a means of getting about. She was anxious not to relinquish all her work in Seaton, but she could not now bear the fatigue of walking. In her car distance was no obstacle, and she could continue her inspection of boarded-out workhouse children, attend babies' clinics in country villages beyond the city area, visit the wives of soldiers and sailors, regulate the orphanage, and superintend the Tipperary Club. Miss Beach's energetic temperament made her miserable unless fully occupied, so, the doctor having forbidden her former strenuous round of duties, she adopted the car as a compromise, assuring him that she would limit her list to a few of her pet schemes only. It was probably her wisest course. It is very hard for elderly people to be laid on the shelf, and to feel that their services are set aside. Miss Beach had lived so entirely in her various philanthropic occupations, that to give everything up would have been a severe mental shock. As it was, she managed to obey medical orders, and at the same time, to a certain extent, keep her old place in the work of the city.

As the days became longer and lighter, she sometimes took her great-niece with her in the car. Winona had really very little time out of school hours; her duties as Games Captain were paramount, and hockey practices and matches absorbed most of her holiday afternoons. When she had an occasional free hour, however, it was an immense treat to go motoring. She loved the feeling of spinning along through the country lanes. It was delightful to see new places and fresh roads. Seaton was in the midst of a beautiful district, and there were charming villages, woods, and lovely views of scenery within easy distance.

One Saturday, when for a wonder there was no event at school, Miss Beach suddenly suggested that they should start in the car, take a luncheon basket with them, and explore some of the country in the neighborhood. It was a glorious spring morning, with a clear pale blue sky, and a touch of warmth in the sunshine that set winter to flight, and brought the buds out on the trees. On such a day the human sap, too, seems to rise, there is an exhilaration, physical and spiritual, when we long to run or to sing for the sheer vital joy of living, when our troubles don't seem to matter, and the future looks rosy, and for the moment we feel transferred to the golden age of the poets, when the world was young, and Pan played his pipes in the meadows among the asphodels. Winona, at any rate, was in an ecstatic frame of mind, and though Aunt Harriet did not openly express her enthusiasm, the mere fact of her suggesting such an outing proved that the spring had called her, and that she was ready to go out and worship at Nature's shrine. Do not imagine for a moment that Miss Beach, whatever her feelings, allowed any romantic element to appear on the surface. She fussed over the car, measured the amount of petrol left in the tank, debated whether she had better go to the garage for an extra can in case of emergencies, called out the cook to dust the seat, sent the housemaid flying to the attic for an air-cushion, inspected the lunch basket, gave half-a-dozen directions for things to be done in her absence, wrote last messages on a slate for people who might possibly call on business, scolded Winona for putting on her thin coat, and sent her to fetch her thick one and a rug for her knees, and

Angela Brazil

finally, after a very breathless ten minutes got under way, and started forth. They drove slowly through the town traffic, but soon they had left streets behind, and were spinning along the high road in the direction of Wickborough.

Long as she had lived at Seaton, Miss Beach had never seen Wickborough Castle, and to-day she was determined to pay it a visit. It was a very ancient place, built originally by King Canute, in the days when red war was waged between Saxon and Norseman. Little of the old Danish tower remained, but successive generations had erected keep and turret, bastion and guard house, crumbling now indeed into ruins, but picturesque in their decay, and full of historical associations. Here proud Queen Margaret, hard pressed by her enemies, had found a timely shelter for herself and her little son, till an escort could convey her to a spot of greater safety; here Richard II. had pursued sweet unwilling Anne of Warwick, and forced her to accept his hated suit; Princess Mary had passed a part of her unhappy childhood within its walls, and Anne Boleyn's merry laugh had rung out there. The situation of the Castle was magnificent. It stood on the summit of a wooded cliff which ran sheer into the river, and commanded a splendid prospect of the country round, and a bird's-eye view of the little town that clustered at the foot of the crag.

"It's like an eagle's nest!" commented Winona, as leaving the car at the bottom of the hill they climbed on foot up the zigzag pathway to the keep. "It must have been a regular robber-baron's stronghold in the Middle Ages!"

Miss Beach had bought a guide-book, and rejecting the services of a persistent little girl who was anxious to point out the various spots of interest, with an eye to a tip, they strolled about, trying to reconstruct a fancy portrait of the place for themselves. Canute's tower was still left, a squat solid piece of masonry, with enormously thick walls and tiny lancet windows. It was rather dark, but as it was the only portion remaining intact, it was used as a museum, and various curiosities were preserved there. The great fire-place held a spit for roasting an ox whole, and had a poker five feet long; stone cannon-balls were piled up on the floor, and on the walls hung a medieval armory of helmets, gorgelets, breast-plates, coats of mail, shields and swords, daggers and lances. A special feature of the museum was a wax-work figure of a knight clad in full armor which gave an excellent idea of what Sir Bevis of Wickborough must have looked like somewhere about the year 1217. Another figure, dressed in rich velvet and fur, with flowered silk kirtle, represented his wife Dame Philippa, in the act of offering him a silver goblet of wine, while a hound stood with its head pressed to her hand. The group was so natural that it was almost startling, and took the spectator back as nothing else could have done to the ancient medieval days which it pictured. A small stair in the corner of the tower led down to a dungeon, where, lying among the straw, was an equally impressive wax-work figure of a prisoner, wretched, unkempt, and bound hand and foot with chains. A pitcher of water lay by his side, and a stuffed rat peering from the straw added a further touch of realism. Winona shuddered. It was a ghastly sight, and she was thankful to run up the stairs and go from the keep out into the spring sunshine. She had always had a romantic admiration for the Middle Ages, but this aspect of thirteenth-century life did not commend itself to her. "They were bad old times, after all!" she decided, and came to the conclusion that the twentieth century, even with its horrible war, was a more humane period to live in.

At the foot of the crag, close by the river, lay the remains of the old Priory Church, an ivy-covered fabric, whose broken chancel still gave a shelter to the battered tombs of the knights who had lived in the Castle above. Sir Bevis and Dame Philippa lay here in marble, their features calm and rigid, their hands folded in prayer, less human indeed, but infinitely grander than in their wax effigies of the tower. Seven centuries of sunshine and storm had passed over their heads, and castle and church were alike in ruins.

"Their bones are dust,
Their good swords rust,

Their souls are with the Saints, we trust,"

thought Winona, as she took a photograph of the quiet scene. It was deeply interesting, but on this glorious lovely spring day it seemed a little too sad. With all the birds singing, and the hedges in bud, and the daisies showing white stars among the grass, she wanted to live in the present, and not in the past. And yet, if we think about it rightly, the past is never really sad. Those who lived before us accomplished their work, and have passed onwards - a part of the world scheme - to, we doubt not, fuller and worthier work beyond. We, still in the preparatory class of God's great school, cannot yet grasp the higher forms, but those who have been moved up surely smile at our want of comprehension, and look back on this earth as the College undergraduate remembers his kindergarten; for the spiritual evolution goes ever on, working always Godwards, and when the human dross falls away, the imperfect and the partial will be merged into the perfect and the eternal. The broken eggshells may lie in the old nest, but the fledged larks are singing in the blue of the sky.

From the little town of Wickborough they drove along the old Roman road towards Danestone. Part of their way lay across Wickland Heath, and here, as it was now past mid-day, Miss Beach suggested that they should stop and take their lunch. It was a most glorious spot for a picnic. They were at the top of a tableland, and before them spread the Common, a brown sea of last year's heather and bilberry, with gorse bushes flaming here and there like golden fires. A sparrow-hawk, more majestic than any aeroplane, sailed serenely overhead, and a pair of whinchats, perturbed by his vicinity, flew with a sharp twitter over the low stone wall, and sought cover among the brambles. Beyond stretched the Roman road, broad and straight, a landmark for miles. Cities and civilization were far away, and they were alone with the moor and the peaty little brook, and the birds and the sun and the fresh spring wind. The joyous influence was irresistible; even Miss Beach dropped ten years' burden of cares, and waxed almost light-hearted. Winona had seldom seen her aunt in such a mood, and she seized the opportunity as a favorable moment to proffer a request which she had often longed, but had never hitherto dared, to make. It was no less a suggestion than that she might be allowed to try to drive the car. She put it in tentative fashion, fully expecting a refusal, but Aunt Harriet received the idea quite graciously.

"There's no reason why you shouldn't. The road's wide and straight, and not a vehicle in sight; you couldn't have a better place to learn on in the whole of the kingdom. Mind you do exactly what I tell you, that's all!"

Winona's face was shining. Ever since she had first seen the pretty little two-seater it had been her secret ambition to work its steering wheel for herself. She packed up the lunch basket in a hurry, for fear her aunt might repent. But Miss Beach seldom went back on her word, and was quite disposed and ready to act motor instructress. She began by explaining very carefully the various levers, and how to start.

"One golden rule," she urged, "is to take care the lever is at neutral before you begin, or the car will jump on you. Many motorists have had nasty accidents by omitting that most necessary precaution. Next you must see that the ignition is pushed back, or you'll get a back-fire in starting, and break your wrist. It must be just at this notch - do you see? Now you may swing round the handle."

The engine began to work, and Winona took her place in the driver's seat. Miss Beach, sitting by her side, showed her how to put the low gear in, then to put in the clutch. The car started off under Winona's guidance.

She gripped the steering wheel tightly, turning it to right or left at first according to her aunt's directions, but soon from instinctive comprehension. It was something like guiding a gigantic bicycle; she could not yet exactly estimate the amount of turn required, but she felt that it would come to her with practice. There was an immense exhilaration in feeling the car

Angela Brazil

under her control. For a beginner, she really kept very steadily in the middle of the road; occasionally Aunt Harriet made a snatch at the wheel, but that was seldom necessary. They were going very slowly, only about ten miles an hour, but even that seemed a tolerable speed to a novice. The road was curving now, and Winona must steer round a corner; it was easier than she had expected, and her instructress ejaculated "Good!" The sense of balance was beginning to come to her. Such a tiny movement of the wheel sent the car to right or left; at first she had jerked it clumsily, now she could reckon the proportion with greater nicety. Was that something coming in the distance? "Sound your hooter!" shouted Aunt Harriet quickly, as a motor cycle hove in sight. In rather a panic, Winona squeezed the india-rubber bulb, making the car lurch as she took her hand momentarily from the wheel. "Keep well to the left!" commanded Miss Beach, and Winona, with her heart in her mouth, contrived to obey, and passed her first vehicle successfully. She heaved a sigh of relief when it had whizzed by, and the road was once more clear. Naturally, however, she could not expect to keep a thoroughfare all to herself. Further on, she overtook a farmer's cart full of little squealing pigs. As it occupied the exact center of the road she hooted (with great confidence this time), and, when it had swung to the left, she rounded it successfully on the right. A furniture van looked a terrible obstacle, but she passed it without assistance, and began to wax quite courageous. Three motor cars in succession tearing along one after another, and sounding ear-splitting electric hooters, left her nerves rather rocky. When houses and chimneys appeared in sight Miss Beach told her to stop.

"I daren't let a learner drive through a village. There are always too many children and dogs about the street. Change places with me now, and you shall try again when we come to a quiet road."

Rather thankful not to have to venture her 'prentice skill in the narrow winding street, Winona gave the wheel into her aunt's more experienced hands. It was only *pro tem.*, however, for when they were once more in the open country Miss Beach continued the lesson, making her start and stop several times just for practice.

"I believe you know the routine now," she said. "It's the motorist's first catechism. Remember those cardinal rules, and you can't go so far wrong."

"Do experienced people ever forget them?" asked Winona.

"Sometimes, when they grow careless. Mr. Forster sprained his wrist the other day with a back-fire, which he ought to have avoided, and I heard of a horrible accident in Paris, when a chauffeur started his car with the clutch in gear, with the consequence that it dashed over a bridge into the Seine, and the occupants - a lady and two little children - were drowned before his eyes. There's no need to be nervous if you take proper care, but cars are not playthings to be trifled with."

They had reached a part of the country which Miss Beach had known as a child. She had not visited it since, and was interested to see again spots which had once been familiar.

"I remember the river perfectly," she said. "And that hill, with the wood where we used to get blackberries in the autumn. I wonder if the wild daffodils still grow in Chipden Marsh! It's fifty years since I gathered them! Shall we go and see? They ought just to be out now, and it's really not late yet."

Winona was only too delighted to prolong the day's outing, and would not have demurred if Aunt Harriet had proposed returning home by moonlight. She caught eagerly at the suggestion of finding daffodils. Though half-a-century had sped by Miss Beach remembered the way, and drove through many by-lanes to a tract of low-lying pasture land that bordered the river. She had not forgotten the stile, which still remained as of yore, so leaving the car in the road they walked down the fields. At first they were disappointed, but further on, beside the river, the Marsh might well have been called "Daffodil Meadow." Everywhere the lovely little wild Lent lilies were showing their golden trumpets in such profusion among the grass that the scene resembled Botticelli's famous picture of spring. Miss Beach said little, but her eyes shone with reminiscences. Winona was in ecstasies, and ran about picking till her bunch was almost too big to hold. The slanting afternoon sunlight fell on the water with a glinting, glistening sheen; the sallows overhanging the banks were yellow with pollen, the young pushing arum shoots and river herbs wore their tender early spring hue; the scene was an idyll in green and gold. They were loath to leave, but time was passing, so, very reluctantly, they walked up the fields again to rejoin the car. They had stowed their daffodils in the lunch basket, and Winona was peeping over the hedge to take a last look at the river, when an exclamation behind her made her turn round. Miss Beach was leaning heavily against the car, her face was ashen gray, her lips were white and drawn. She looked ready to faint. Winona flew to her in a panic.

"What is it, Aunt Harriet? Are you ill? Get into the car and sit down. Let me help you!"

Miss Beach sank on to the seat, and sat with half-closed eyes, moaning feebly. Winona was terribly alarmed. She had seen Aunt Harriet before with one of her bad heart attacks, and knew that restoratives ought to be given. In this lonely spot, with no help at hand, what was to be done? Suppose her aunt were to faint - die, even, before aid could be rendered? For a moment Winona shook like a leaf. Then, with a rush, her presence of mind returned. There was only one possible course – she herself must start the car, and drive to within reach of civilization. It would need courage! It was one thing to drive with an experienced instructor at her elbow to shout necessary directions, but quite another to manage alone, with Aunt Harriet half unconscious beside her. Suppose she were to forget part of her motorists' catechism, and make some horrible, fatal mistake! Well, it must be ventured, all the same! Every minute's delay was important.

With a nervous shiver she forced herself to action. She looked first that the clutch was out of gear, and that the ignition was pushed back, then swung round the handle to start the engine. It had cooled while they were picking daffodils, and she was obliged to repeat the process four times ere the welcome whirring answered her efforts. She sprang to her seat, took off the brake, and put in the low gear. Then she put the clutch in with her foot. But alas! in her tremor and hurry she had done it too suddenly, and stopped the engine! She could have cried with annoyance at her stupidity. There was nothing for it but to put the lever again at neutral, put on the brake, and climb out to re-swing the handle. This time the engine, being warm, was more amiable and condescended to start easily. Winona leaped into the car, adjusted her levers, put in her clutch more gradually, and the car glided slowly away. With a feeling of desperation she gripped the steering wheel. The lane was narrow and twisting, and not too smooth. Suppose she were to meet a farm cart - could she possibly pass it in safety? She had a feeling that she would run into any vehicle that might approach her. So far the lane was empty, but at any moment an obstacle might arise. What was that? There was a sound of baa-ing, and round a corner ran a flock of sheep, urged on by a boy and a collie dog. Here was the first human being she had seen, and for a second she thought of stopping to ask for help. But what could a stupid-looking young boy do for her? No, it were better far to push on. She managed to sound the hooter, and with a supreme effort kept in the middle of the lane, while the sheep scattered to right and left. She dared not go any slower, for fear of stopping her engine, but she expected every instant to feel a bump, and find that she had run over one of the flock. The collie did his duty, however, and in a whirl of barking, shouting, and baa-ing she steered safely through the danger.

She looked anxiously at every turning, for fear she might miss her way. Her object was to regain the main road, where she might find some passing motorist, and implore help. Yes, there was the sign-post where Aunt Harriet had halted, she must keep to the left by that ruined cottage - she remembered noticing its broken roof as they had passed it. How interminably long the lanes were! They had seemed far shorter when Aunt Harriet was driving! Oh! thank goodness, there was the big oak tree - it could not be far now. A few minutes more and Winona had reached the sign-post, and swung round the corner into the Crowland Road. She felt as if her nerves would not stand very much more. Would help never come? A distant hooting behind her made her heart leap. She stopped the car beside the hedge, and standing up, waved her handkerchief as a signal of distress. A splendid Daimler came into sight. Would the chauffeur notice and understand her plight? She shrieked in desperation as it whizzed past. Oh! It was stopping! A gentleman got out, and walked quickly back towards her. She jumped down, and ran to meet him.

"Can I be of any assistance?" he asked politely.

"Oh, please! My aunt is very ill, and I don't know how to drive properly yet. How am I going to get back to Seaton?" blurted out Winona, on the verge of tears.

She never forgot how kind the stranger was. With the aid of his chauffeur he lifted poor Aunt Harriet into his own car, and told Winona to take her place beside her.

"Now tell me exactly where you want to go," he said, "and I'll run you straight home as fast as I can. My man shall follow with your car. You can manage this little two-seater, Jones?"

"Yes, Sir," grinned the chauffeur, inspecting the levers.

The stranger made his big Daimler fly. Winona never knew by how much he exceeded the speed limit, but it seemed to her that they must be spinning along at the rate of nearly fifty miles an hour. Aunt Harriet had recovered a little, though she still moaned at intervals. The hedges seemed to whirl past them, they went hooting through villages, and whizzed over a common. At last the familiar spires and towers of Seaton appeared in the distance. Their good Samaritan drove them to their own door, helped Miss Beach into the house, and volunteered to take a message to the doctor, then, evading Winona's thanks, he sprang into his car, and started away.

The chauffeur arrived later with Miss Beach's car, and considerately offered to run it round to the garage.

Aunt Harriet was laid up for several days after this episode, and Dr. Sidwell forbade any long expeditions in the immediate future. He encouraged the idea of Winona learning to drive.

"You could be of the greatest help in taking your aunt about," he said to her. "You must have a capital notion of it, or you couldn't have brought the car three miles entirely on your own. But of course you'll need practice before you can be trusted to mix in traffic. You'll have to apply for a license, remember. You'll be getting into trouble if you drive without!"

Winona looked back upon that outing as a most memorable occasion. She hoped to try her skill again as soon as opportunity offered. The charm of the wheel was alluring. She wished she knew the name of the stranger who had rendered such invaluable assistance. But that she never learnt.

Angela Brazil

CHAPTER XVI

THE ATHLETIC DISPLAY

The Easter term was passing quickly away. It had been a strenuous but nevertheless successful season. Out of nine hockey matches the team had lost only three - not a bad record for a school that was still in the infancy of its Games reputation. The Old Girls' Guild had got up its eleven, and had practiced with enthusiasm under the captaincy of Kirsty Paterson. A most exciting Past *versus* Present match had been played, resulting in a narrow victory for the school. Winona felt prouder of this success than of any other triumph the team had scored, for Kirsty had congratulated her afterwards, and praise from her former captain was very sweet. It had been the last match of the season, so it made a satisfactory finish to her work. She felt quite sentimental as she put by her hockey-stick. Next season there would be a fresh captain, and she would have left the High School! She wished she were staying another year, but her scholarship would expire at the end of July. She could hardly believe that she had been nearly two years at the school, and that only one term more remained to her. Well, it would be the summer term, which was the pleasantest of all, and though hockey was over, she had the cricket season before her. The Seaton High should score at the wicket if it were in her power to coach a successful team.

Towards the end of March Winona had an interlude which for the time took her thoughts even from the omnipresent topic of sports. Percy, who had been in training with his regiment at

Duncastle, was ordered to the Front. He was allowed thirty-six hours' leave, and came home for a Sunday. Winona spent that week-end at Highfield, and the memory of it always remained a very precious one. Percy in his khaki seemed much changed, and though she only had him for a few minutes quite to herself, she felt that the old tie between them had strengthened. Her letters to him in future would be different. During the last year they had both slacked a little in their correspondence, each perhaps unconsciously feeling that the other's standpoint was changing; now they had met again on a new basis, and realized once more a common bond of sympathy. Percy, absorbed in describing his new life, scarcely mentioned Aunt Harriet. The episode of the burning of the paper seemed to have faded from his memory, or he had conveniently buried it in oblivion. Winona had never forgotten it. It remained still the one shadow in her career at Seaton. Now especially, since Miss Beach's recent ill-health, the secret weighed heavily upon her. She felt her aunt ought to know that the will was destroyed, so that she might take the opportunity of making another. More than once she tried indirectly to refer to the subject, but it was a tender topic, and at the least hint Miss Beach's face would stiffen and her voice harden; the old barrier between them would rise up again wider than ever, and impossible to be spanned. Winona would have been glad to do much for her aunt, but Miss Beach did not care to be treated as an invalid. Like many energetic people, she refused to acknowledge that she was ill, and the acceptance of little services seemed to her a confession of her own weakness. It is rather hard to have your kindly meant efforts repulsed, so Winona, finding that her offers of sympathy met with no response, drew back into her shell, and the two continued to live as before, on terms of friendship but never of intimacy. After almost two years spent in the same house Winona knew her aunt little better than on the day of her arrival. They had certain common grounds for conversation, but their mutual reserve was maintained, and as regarded each other's real thoughts they remained "strangers yet."

Angela Brazil

Miss Beach, however, took an interest in Winona's doings at school. She read her monthly reports, and scolded her if her work had fallen below standard. She expressed a guarded pleasure over successful matches, but rubbed in the moral that games must not usurp her attention to the detriment of her form subjects.

"You came here to learn something more than hockey!" she would remind Winona. "It's a splendid exercise, but I'm afraid it won't prove a career! I should like to see a better record for Latin and Chemistry; they might very well have more attention!"

Winona had tried to persuade her aunt to come and watch one of the matches, but Miss Beach had always found some engagement; she was concerned in so many of the city's activities that her time was generally carefully mapped out weeks beforehand. She consented, however, to accept Miss Bishop's invitation to the Gymnasium Display, which was to be given at the High School at the close of the Easter term.

This was a very important occasion in the estimation of the girls. It was their first athletic show since the advent of Miss Barbour, the Swedish drill mistress. Governors and parents were to be present, and the excellence of the performance must justify the large amount which had been spent upon gymnastic apparatus during the past year.

For two whole terms Miss Barbour had been teaching and training her classes with a view to this exhibition, and woe betide any unlucky wight whose nerves, memory or muscles should fail her at the critical moment! A further impetus was given to individual effort by the offer, on the part of one of the Governors, of four medals for competition, to be awarded respectively to the best candidates in four classes, Seniors over 16, Intermediates from 13 to 16, Juniors from 10 to 13, and Preparatories under 10. It was felt throughout the school that the offer was munificent. The Governors had been stingy over the matter of the hockey field, and had been reviled accordingly, but Councillor Jackson was retrieving the character of the Board by this action, and the girls reversed their opinion in his favor. They hoped that other Governors, warmed by his example, might open their hearts in silver medals or book prizes for future occasions.

"He's a dear old trump to think of it!" said Winona.

"You drew a picture of him floundering in the mud at hockey!" twinkled Garnet.

"Well, I forgive him now, and I'll draw another of him standing on the platform, all beaming with benevolence, and distributing medals broadcast. Look here, Bessie Kirk, you needn't be congratulating yourself beforehand with such a patently self-satisfied smirk, because *I'm* going to win the Senior Medal."

"No, you're not, my child! Take it patiently, and compose your mind. The medal's coming this way!"

"How about me?" put in Marjorie Kemp.

"You'll do well, but you're not a champion! You're too fat, Jumbo, and that's the fact. You're all right when it's a question of brute strength, but when agility matters, those superfluous pounds of flesh of yours are an impediment. I'd back Joyce sooner than you; she's as light as a feather!"

Hearing herself commended, Joyce fluttered up to the group, smiling.

"I did four feet six, yesterday," she announced, "and I'd have cleared four feet seven, I believe, only I had to stop. It's always my luck!"

"Why had you to stop?"

"My back ached!"

Instant apprehension overspread the faces of her friends.

"Joyce Newton!" exclaimed Winona, "you're never going to get small-pox again, and stop the athletic display?"

"You don't feel sick, or head-achy, or sore-throaty, do you?" implored Bessie. "For goodness sake stand away, if you're infectious! I don't want to be another contact case!"

"What pigs you are!" said Joyce plaintively, "One can't catch small-pox twice!"

"But you might be going to get scarlet fever, or measles, or even influenza!"

"Stop ragging! Mayn't I have a back-ache if I want? It's my own back!"

"Have as many back-aches as you choose, my hearty, but don't disseminate germs! If the athletic display doesn't come off, I'll break my heart, and you can write an epitaph over me:

"Here lies one who young in years,
Left this mortal vale of tears;
Cruel fate hath knocked her down,
Tom from her the laurel crown,
To win the gym display she sighed,
But as she might not jump, she died!"

"Look here!" said Marjorie. "I suppose the medal lies fairly well between us four. I vote that we make a compact - whoever wins treats the other three to ices! It would be some compensation for losing!"

"Good for you, Jumbo! I'm game!" agreed Bessie.

"If you'll undertake they'll be strawberry ices!" stipulated Winona.

"I mayn't eat ices, they disagree with me!" wailed Joyce, "but if you'll make it chocolates."

"Done! I won't forget. Ices for Bessie and Winona, and a packet of Cadbury's for Joyce. I'll go and be ordering them!" chirruped Marjorie, dancing away.

"Cheek! Don't make so sure."

"It's *my* medal, so be getting your handkerchiefs ready," maintained Winona.

Though Winona, just for the fun of teasing her friends, had pretended to appropriate the prize, she had really no anticipation of winning. She was fairly good at gymnasium work, but could not be considered a champion. She knew her success or failure would depend very much on luck. If she happened to feel in the right mood she might achieve something, but it was an even chance that at the critical moment her courage might fail her. In a match she was generally swept away by the intense feeling of cooperation, the knowledge that all her team were striving for a common cause buoyed her up, but in a competition where each was for herself, the element of nervousness would have greater scope. When she thought about it, she felt that she would probably be shaking with fright.

The great day came at last. The Gymnasium was decorated with flags in honor of the occasion, and pots of palms were placed upon the platform where the Governors and a few of the most distinguished visitors were accommodated with seats. Winona, marching in to take part in the senior drill, gave one glance round the building, and grasped the fact that Aunt Harriet was sitting on the platform next to Councillor Jackson, and only a few places away from the expert who was to act as judge. She was chatting affably with her august companions. Think of chatting with a Governor! Winona felt that it was some credit to have such a relation! She had not always been very sure how much she valued Aunt Harriet's opinion, but this afternoon she longed to shine before her. Yet the very wish to do so made her nervous. She glanced at her companions. Bessie was looking stolidity itself, Marjorie's usually high color had reached peony point, Joyce was palpably in the throes of stage fright. All were soon marching and countermarching, swinging Indian clubs, and performing the intricate maneuvers of Swedish drill. Fortunately they had practiced well, and it went without a hitch. They breathed more freely as they retired to the ante-room to make way for the babies who were to do skipping exercises to music.

"It's more awful to show off before Governors than I expected!" sighed Joyce. "I'm just shivering!"

"What'll you be at the rings, then?" asked Bessie.

"Silence!" urged Miss Lever, who was in charge of the ante-room.

The strains of "Little Grey Home in the West" and the regular thud of small feet were wafted from the gymnasium.

"Don't you wish you were a kid again?" whispered Joyce.

"No, I don't!" retorted Bessie, so imprudently loud that Miss Lever glared at her.

"It's horrid having to stay in here, where one can't see!" murmured Marjorie under her breath.

They knew by the music, however, what was taking place. The juniors were doing wand exercises, the intermediates followed with clubs.

"Our turn again soon," whispered Winona.

Olave Parry, from a vantage post near the door, could see into the gymnasium, and report progress. Her items of news passed in whispers down the ranks. The babies had skipped like a row of cherubs, and the Governors were wreathed in smiles. Kitty Carter had dropped one of her clubs, and it nearly hit a visitor on the head, but fortunately missed her by half an inch. Laura Marshall was performing prodigies on the horizontal ladder - she undoubtedly had a chance for a medal. Bursts of applause from the audience punctuated the performance. Olave continued her report, which Miss Lever, who took occasional excursions into the gymnasium, verified from time to time. The juniors were competing now. Natalie Powers was about to do the ring exercises. It was a swing and a pull-up in front, and she managed that neatly, but when it came to the swing and the turn, she lost her nerve, turned too soon and spun round helplessly in the air until Miss Barbour hurried to her aid. Natalie was done for, without doubt! It was a good thing she had not fallen and hurt herself. Her rivals were rope-climbing. Madge Collins had reached the top in six seconds, and was sliding down again, to the accompaniment of loud clapping. Lennie Roberts had beaten her, for she had performed the same feat in exactly five seconds. The juniors were in a ferment of excitement. The interest of the audience had waxed to enthusiasm point.

"Seniors!" announced Miss Lever briefly, and the row of waiting figures in the ante-room fell into line, and marched into the gymnasium for the special trials. The Swedish drill exercises, where all worked together, had not seemed half so formidable. A well practiced part is not easily forgotten even by a nervous girl, if it must be done in company with others. It was another matter, however, to perform single athletic feats before a big audience. For a moment Winona turned almost dizzy with fright. The big room seemed full of eyes, every one of which would be watching her when it came to her turn. She looked round with the feeling of a martyr in the arena, and for a moment met the calm steady gaze of Miss Beach. Winona said afterwards that Aunt Harriet must have mesmerized her, for in that second of recognition she felt a sudden rush of courage. The thrill of the contest took possession of her, and every nerve and muscle, every atom of her brain, was alert to do its best. She would let Aunt Harriet see that, though she might fail sometimes in form work, she could hold her own at gymnastics.

Contestants climbed, traveled on rings, and vaulted the horse. Winona seemed to herself as easy and agile as she had ever been. She had a possible chance of winning, and her heart exulted. Then came the ladders. Up and up she went, holding herself now by her hands and now by her feet swinging for her hold. She had thought she was light, but now she suddenly realized how heavy she was! She summoned every bit of strength as she went down the ladder. From one contest to another she passed, doing her best.

Last of all came the rings. Winona swung out, grasped the next ring, and so on down the line. Oh, how many there were! She had never before realized what it meant to weigh 7 st. 10 lbs. She held her breath as she reached for the next ring, but it slipped from her fingers. Only for a second, however, for she caught it on the next swing, and a moment later was waiting at the end. Bessie was just starting. Down the line she traveled, not so gracefully, perhaps, as Winona, but catching her ring on every swing. Joyce followed, but mid-way her courage deserted her, and she failed utterly. Marjorie came next. She was doing well surely! She was nearly through, reached for the last ring, missed it, and fell! There was an instant murmur of consternation from the audience. Was she injured? She sprang up unhurt, however, though deeply humiliated.

Thrilling in every nerve, Winona started back. Refreshed by her little rest, she swung lightly, steadily and unfalteringly, never missing a ring till she came to the end. She was almost too occupied to notice the cheers. Bessie reached mid-way, then missed a ring, caught it on the second swing, missed another, and reached for it three times before she caught it and finished her course.

The girls had been too much excited for comparisons. They scarcely guessed how their averages would stand. Winona had a general impression that Bessie had scored at vaulting, and

Marjorie had undoubtedly cleared the rope at four feet eight. Her own performances seemed lost in a haze; she had noticed the judge jot down something, but she felt incapable of reckoning her chances.

The judge was conferring with Miss Bishop at the back of the platform, and while the room waited for their decision the school marched, singing an Empire song.

At last the judge stepped to the front of the platform. The singing ceased. Winona's heart beat suffocatingly.

"I have great pleasure in giving the results," announced the judge. "Preparatory prize, Elaine Jennings; Junior prize, Lennie Roberts; Intermediate prize, Laura Marshall; Senior prize, Winona Woodward."

The applause was ringing out lustily. Bessie, Marjorie and Joyce were pressing congratulations upon her. Miss Bishop (actually the Head!) was looking at her and smiling approval. Miss Lever was telling her to walk forward. In a delirious whirl, Winona climbed the steps on the platform. As Councillor Jackson pinned the medal on to her tunic, a storm of clapping and cheers rose from the school. Their Games Captain was popular, and everybody felt it right and fitting that this afternoon she should have proved herself the athletic champion.

"Don't forget the ices!" whispered Bessie, as Winona rejoined Marjorie and Joyce.

"We'll stop at the cafe on the way home, and you shall each choose what you like!" declared Winona, with spendthrift liberality.

CHAPTER XVII

BACK TO THE LAND

Easter fell late, so Winona spent the lovely early part of May at her own home. After so many weeks of town it was delightful to be once more in the country. She worked with enthusiasm in the garden, mowed the lawn, and with Letty and Mamie's help began to put up an arbor, over which she hoped to persuade a crimson rambler to ramble successfully. In the house she tried her hand at scones and cakes, entirely to the children's satisfaction, if not altogether to her own; she enjoyed experiments in cooking, for she had longed to join the Domestic Science class at school, and had felt aggrieved when Miss Bishop decided that her time-table was full enough without it. She found her mother looking delicate and worried. Poor Mrs. Woodward's health had not improved during the last two years; she was nervous, anxious about Percy, and inclined to be fretful and tearful. The increased income-tax and the added cost of living made her constantly full of financial cares; she was not a very good manager, and the thought of the future oppressed her.

"I don't know what's to be done with you, Winona, when you leave school!" she remarked plaintively one evening. "I feel that you ought to go in for something, but I'm sure I don't know what! I'd hoped you were going to turn out clever, and win a scholarship for College, and get a good post as a teacher afterwards, but there doesn't seem the least chance of your doing that. It's all very well this hockey and cricket that's made such a fuss of at schools nowadays, but it doesn't seem to me that it's going to lead to anything. I'd rather you stuck to your books! Yes, your future's worrying me very much. I've all these little ones to bring up and educate, and I'd hoped you'd be able to earn your own living before long, and lend the children a helping hand. I can't spend anything on giving you an expensive training, Percy has cost me so much out of capital, and it's Letty's turn next, besides which it's high time Ernie and Godfrey were packed off to a boarding-school. Oh, dear! I never seem free from trouble! It's no light anxiety to be the mother of seven children! I often wonder what will become of you all!"

To Winona her mother's tearful confidences came as a shock. Up to the present she had been so intensely interested in school affairs that she had given scarcely a thought to her future career. Life had existed for her in detail only to the end of the summer term, after that it had stretched a nebulous void into which her imagination had never troubled to penetrate. Now she took herself seriously to task, and tried to face the prospect of the time when she would have left the Seaton High School. There were many occupations open to girls nowadays besides teaching; they could be doctors, secretaries, sanitary inspectors, artists, musicians, poultry farmers. She knew however, that for any career worth taking up a considerable training would be necessary, and a certain amount of expense involved. What she would have liked very much would be to study at a Physical Training College, and qualify to become a Drill and Games Mistress, but this seemed as unattainable as taking a medical course or going to Girton or Newnham.

"I'm too young yet for a hospital nurse," she pondered, "and not clever enough to be an artist or a musician. Well, I suppose I can make munitions, or go on the land! Women are wanted on farms while the war lasts. I could earn my own living, perhaps. But oh, dear! That wouldn't be boosting on the children! I'm afraid mother's fearfully disappointed with me."

She seemed to be looking at things in a new light, and to see

Angela Brazil

her position as it affected others. She was young and brave; surely it was her part to shoulder the family burdens, to shield the frail little mother who grew less and less able to cope with difficulties, to hold out a strong helping hand to the younger brothers and sisters, and so justify her existence on this planet. It had not before occurred to her how much her home people relied on her. The thought of it brought a great lump into her throat. She must not fail them. She could not yet see her way clearly, but somehow she must be a comfort and a support to them, that she was quite resolved.

She went back to school in a very thoughtful frame of mind. Her last term would be a full one in many ways. About half of the Sixth Form were to go in for their college entrance examinations, and Miss Bishop had decreed that Winona, as a County Scholarship holder, must certainly be among the number. She had little hope of passing, for most of her subjects were weak, but she meant to make an effort to try to pick up some of her lost ground. Her old enemies, Latin and Chemistry, still often baffled her, and her memory was only moderately retentive. She could not honestly believe that so far as her work was concerned she was any credit to the school. Games were another matter, however, and so long as they did not seriously interfere with her preparation for the matriculation, she meant to do her duty as captain. She arranged cricket fixtures and tennis tournaments, and though she could not devote as much of her own time as she would have liked to practice, she spurred on others who had more leisure than herself. She certainly possessed a gift for organization. There are some captains, splendid players themselves, who can never train their deputies. As Napoleon's genius was supposed to lie largely in his capacity for picking out able generals, so Winona proved her ability by choosing helpers who were of real service to her. With Audrey Redfern, Emily Cooper, and Bertha March to the fore, she hoped that both cricket and tennis would prosper, and that the school would score as successfully during the summer as it had done in the hockey season.

On the first Saturday after the beginning of the term, Miss

Beach announced that she was going to spend the day with a friend who lived five miles out of Seaton, and that if Winona had leisure to accompany her she would be pleased to take her. No practices had been arranged for that afternoon, so Winona felt free to accept the invitation. She had been for several short runs in the car, but for no long expedition since the memorable outing to Wickborough, so the prospect of a day in the country was alluring.

They started at about eleven o'clock, and took a road that was new to Winona, consequently all the more interesting. Their way led through lovely woods, at present a sheet of blue hyacinths, the hedges were a filmy dream of blackthorn blossom, while the swallows wheeling and flashing in the sunshine testified to the return of summer.

Miss Carson, the lady whom they were going to visit, like most of Aunt Harriet's friends was engaged in very interesting work. She had taken a small holding, and with the help of a few women pupils was running it as a fruit, flower and poultry farm. The house, an old cottage, to which she had added a wing, was charmingly pretty. It was long and low, with a thick thatched roof, and a porch overgrown with starry white clematis. A budding vine covered the front and in the border below great clumps of stately yellow lilies drooped their queenly heads. The front door led straight into the house place, a square room with a big fire-place and cozy ingle nooks. It was very simply furnished, but looked most artistic with its rush-bottomed chairs, its few good pictures, and its stained green table with the big bowl of wallflowers.

Miss Carson, a delightfully energetic lady whose age may have been somewhere between thirty and forty, welcomed them cordially.

"I don't apologize for the plainness of my establishment," she remarked. "It's all part of a purpose. We have no servants here, and as we have to do our own house-work in addition to our farm-work, we want to reduce our labor to a minimum. You see, there's hardly anything to dust in this room: the books and the china are in those two cupboards with glass doors, and we have no fripperies at all lying about. The only ornament we allow ourselves is the bowl of flowers. Our bedrooms are equally simple, and our kitchen is fitted with the latest and most up-to-date labor-saving appliances. One of my students is preparing the dinner there now. She's a nice girl, and Winona will perhaps like to go and talk to her, unless she prefers to stay here with us."

Winona promptly decided in favor of the kitchen, so Miss Carson escorted her there, and introduced her to Miss Heald, a jolly-looking girl of about twenty, who, enveloped in a blue overall pinafore, was putting plates to heat, and inspecting the contents of certain boilerettes and casseroles. Like the sitting-room the kitchen contained no unnecessary articles. It was spotlessly clean, and looked very business-like.

"We go on kitchen duty for a week at a time," explained Miss Heald to Winona. "It's a part of the course, you know. We have dairy, gardening and poultry as well. Which do I like best? It's hard to say. Poultry, I think, because the chickens are such darlings. I'll show you all round the place this afternoon, when I've finished washing up. I'm going to lay the table now. You can help if you like."

Precisely at one o'clock the seven other students came in from their work. Each was dressed in her farm uniform, short serge skirt, woolen jersey, blue overall and thick boots. To judge from their looks, their occupation was both healthy and congenial, in physique they were Hebes, and their spirits seemed at bubbling point. Apparently they all adored Miss Carson. The latter made a few inquiries as to the morning's progress, and the capable answers testified to the knowledge of the learners. The dinner did credit to Miss Heald's skill; it was well cooked and daintily served. Winona was full of admiration; her culinary experience was limited so far to cakes and scones; she felt that she would have been very proud if she had compounded that stew, and baked those custards. When the meal was finished the students tramped forth again to their outdoor labor, while Miss Heald cleared away. Winona begged to be allowed to help her, and was initiated into the mysteries of the very latest and most sanitary method of washing up, with the aid of mop, dish-rack, and some patent appliances. It was so interesting that she quite enjoyed it. She swept the kitchen, filled kettles at the pump, and did several other odd jobs; then, everything being left in an absolutely immaculate condition, Miss Heald declared that she was ready, and offered to take her companion for a tour of inspection round the farm.

The little holding had been well planned, and was skillfully arranged. In front was the garden, a large piece of ground stretching down to the hedge that bordered the road. Miss Carson's original idea had been the culture of flowers, partly for the sale of their blossoms, and partly for the preservation of their seeds, but the national need of producing food crops during the war had induced her to plant almost the whole of it with fruit and vegetables. At present it somewhat resembled a village allotment. Patches of peas and broad beans were coming up well. Groups of gooseberry bushes were thriving. Strawberry beds were being carefully weeded, and two of the students were erecting posts round them, over which nets would be hung later on to protect the fruit from the birds.

"Birds are our greatest pest here," explained Miss Heald. "One may like them from a natural history point of view, but you get to hate the little wretches when you see them devouring everything wholesale. They've no conscience. Those small coletits can creep through quite fine meshes, and simply strip the peas, and the blackbirds would guzzle all day if they had the chance. I want to borrow an air gun and pot at them, but Miss Carson won't let me. She's afraid I might shoot some of the other students."

A row of cucumber frames and some greenhouses stood at the bottom of the garden. The latter were mostly devoted to young tomato plants, though one was specially reserved for vegetable marrows. The students had to learn how to manage and regulate the heating apparatus of the houses, as well as to understand the culture of the plants.

"I left a window open once," confessed Miss Heald. "I remembered it when I had been about an hour in bed, and I jumped up and dressed in a hurry, and went out with a lantern to shut it. Fortunately there was no frost that night, or all the seedlings might have been killed. It was a most dreadful thing to forget! I thought Miss Carson would have jumped on me, but she was ever so nice about it."

Despite the predominance of foodstuffs there were a few flowers in the garden, clumps of forget-me-not and narcissus, purple iris, golden saxifrages and scarlet anemones. There were fragrant bushes of lavender and rosemary, and beds of sweet herbs, thyme, and basil and fennel and salsafy, for Miss Carson believed in some of the old-fashioned remedies, and made salves and ointments and hair washes from the products of her garden. The orchard, full of pink-blossomed apple trees, was a refreshing sight. They opened a little gate, and walked under a wealth of drooping flowers to the poultry yard that lay at the further side. Everything here was on the most up-to-date system. Pens of beautiful white Leghorns, Black Minorcas and Buff Orpingtons were kept in wired inclosures, each with its own henhouse and scratching-shed full of straw. Miss Heald took Winona inside to inspect the patent nesting-boxes, and the grit-cutting machine. She also showed her the incubators.

"They're empty now, but you should have seen them in the early spring, when they were full of eggs," she explained. "It was a tremendous anxiety to keep the lamps properly regulated. Miss Nelson and I sat up all night once when some prize ducklings were hatching. It was cold weather, and they weren't very strong, so they needed a little help. It's the most frightfully delicate work to help a chick out of its shell! It makes a little chip with its beak, and then sometimes it can't get any further, and you have gently to crack the hole bigger. Unless you're very careful you may kill it, but on the other hand, if it can't burst its shell when it's ready to hatch, it may suffocate, so it's a choice of evils. We put them in the drying pen first, and then in the 'foster mother.' They're like babies, and have to be fed every two hours. It's a tremendous business when you have hundreds of them, at different stages and on different diets. We seemed to be preparing food all day long. It's ever so fascinating, though!"

"I love them when they're like fluffy canaries," said Winona.

"Yes, so do I. I had a special sitting of little ducklings under my charge, and they got very tame. I put them into a basket one day, and carried them into the garden to pick up worms. I put them down on a bed, and while my back was turned for a few minutes they cleared a whole row of young cabbages that Miss Morrison had just planted. I got into fearful trouble, and had to pack up my *proteges* and take them back to their coop in disgrace. I'd never dreamed they would devour green stuff! We have to learn to keep strict accounts of the poultry; we put down the number of eggs daily, and the weekly food bill, and the chickens sold, and make a kind of register, with profit and loss. Miss Carson runs everything on a most business-like basis."

Miss Heald showed Winona the store-room, where meal and grain were kept, the big pans in which food was mixed, the boxes for packing eggs, and the little medicine cupboard containing remedies for sick fowls. All was beautifully orderly and well arranged, and a card of rules for the help of the students hung on the walls.

From the poultry department they passed to the Dairy Section. The four sleek cows were out in the field, but in a loose box there were some delightful calves that ran to greet Miss Heald, pressing eager damp noses into her hand, and exhibiting much apparent disappointment that she did not offer them a pailful of milk and oatmeal. Winona inspected the cool, scrupulously clean dairy, with its patent churn, and slate slabs for making up the butter. She saw the bowls where the cream was kept, and the wooden print with which the pats were marked.

"Butter-making is the side of the business I don't care for," admitted Miss Heald. "I like the gardening fairly well, and I just love the poultry, but I don't take to dairy work. Of course it's a part of my training, so I'm obliged to do it, but when my time here is over, I mean to make hens my specialty, and go in for poultry farming. An open-air life suits me. It's a thousand times nicer than being a nurse at a hospital, or a secretary at an office. You're in the fresh air all day, and the chicks are so interesting."

A pen of young turkey poults, a flock of goslings, and a sty full of infant pigs were next on exhibition. Miss Heald showed off the latter with pride.

"They're rather darlings, and I own to a weakness for them," she admitted. "We put them in a bath and scrub them, and they're really so intelligent. Wasn't it the poet Herrick who had a pet pig? This little chap's as sharp as a needle. I believe I could teach him tricks directly, if I tried! Miss Carson says I mustn't let myself grow too fond of all the creatures, because their ultimate end is bacon or the boilerette, and it doesn't do to be sentimental over farming; but I can't help it! I just love some of the chickens; they come flying up on to my shoulder like pigeons."

A rough-coated pony formed part of the establishment. Twice a week he was harnessed to the trap, and Miss Carson and one of the students drove to Seaton to dispose of the farm produce. Miss Carson had undertaken to supply several hotels and restaurants with eggs, fowls and vegetables, and so far had found the demand for her goods exceeded the supply. Labor was at present her greatest difficulty. Her students accomplished the light work, but could not do heavy digging. She managed to secure the occasional services of a farm hand, but with most able-bodied men at the war the problem of trenching or of making an asparagus bed was almost impossible to solve.

At the end of the orchard, against a south hedge of thick holly, stood the hives. Bee-keeping was one of the most successful ventures of the holding. Last autumn had shown a splendid yield of honey, and this year, judging by the activity of the bees, an equal harvest might be expected. There was continuous humming among the apple blossoms, and every minute pollen-laden workers were hurrying home with their spoils. Miss Heald lifted the lid of one of the hives, to show Winona the comb within. She observed caution, however.

"They don't know me very well," she explained. "They have their likes and dislikes. Miss Hunter can let them crawl all over her hands and arms, and they never sting her. She must have a natural attraction for them. They recognize a stranger directly. No, I'm not particularly fond of them. I prefer pigs and chickens."

Miss Carson and Aunt Harriet had also been going the round of the farm, and came up to inspect the hives. Miss Beach was greatly interested in her friend's work, and full of congratulations.

"Such women as you are the backbone of the country!" she declared. "The next best thing to fighting is to provide food for the nation. England is capable of producing twice her annual yield if there is proper organization. I'm a great advocate of small holdings, and I think women can't show their patriotism better than by going 'back to the land.' You and your students are indeed 'doing your bit'! You make me want to come and help you!"

It was such a delicious warm afternoon that chairs were carried outside, and they had tea in the garden under a gorgeous pink-blossomed almond tree, with the perfume of wallflowers and sweet scented stocks wafted from the rockery above. Two cats and a dog joined the party, also an impudent bantam cock, who, being considered the mascot of the establishment, was much petted, and allowed certain privileges. He would sit on Miss Carson's wrist like a little tame hawk, and she sometimes brought him into the garden at tea-time to give him tit-bits.

Angela Brazil

At 4.30 all the fowls and chickens were fed, a tremendous business, at which Winona looked on with enthusiasm. She admired the systematic way in which the food was measured and distributed so that each individual member of the flock received its due share, and was not robbed by a greedier and stronger neighbor. She was very reluctant to leave when Miss Beach at last brought round the car.

"How I'd love to go and learn farming when I leave school!" she ventured to remark as they drove home.

"It needs brains!" returned Aunt Harriet, rather snappily. "You mustn't imagine it's all tea in the garden and playing with fluffy chickens. To run such a holding intelligently requires a clever capable head. Your examination's quite enough for you to think about at present. If you're to have any chance at all of passing, it will take your whole energies, I assure you!"

Winona, duly snubbed, held her peace.

CHAPTER XVIII

A FRIEND IN NEED

Under the coaching of Miss Goodson the Sixth Form had settled down to grim work. Twelve girls were to present themselves for examination for entering Dunningham University, and though the teacher naturally concentrated her greatest energies on this elect dozen, the rest by no means slipped through her intellectual net. There were stars among the candidates of whom she might feel moderately certain, and there were also laggers whose success was doubtful. In this latter category she classed Winona. Poor Winona still floundered rather hopelessly in some of her subjects. A poetic imagination may be a delightful inheritance and a source of infinite enjoyment to its owner, but it does not supply the place of a good memory. Examiners are prosaic beings who require solid facts, and even the style of a Macaulay or a Carlyle would not satisfy them unless accompanied by definite answers to their set questions. By a piece of unparallcled luck, Winona had secured and retained her County Scholarship, but her powers of essay writing were not likely to serve her in such good stead again. She often groaned when she thought of the examinations. Miss Bishop, Aunt Harriet, and her mother would all be so disappointed if she failed, and alas! her failure seemed only too probable.

"Miss Goodson doesn't tell me plump out that I'll be plucked, but I can see she thinks so!" confided Winona to Garnet one day.

Angela Brazil

"Then show her she is wrong!"

"Not much chance of that, I'm afraid, but I'm doing my level best. I get up at six every morning, and slave before breakfast."

"So do I, but I get such frightful headaches," sighed Garnet. "I've been nearly mad with them. My cousin took me to the doctor yesterday. He says it's my eyes. I shan't be at school to-morrow. I have to go to Dunningham to see a specialist."

"Poor old girl! You never told me about your headaches."

"You never asked me! I've seen so little of you lately;"

Winona's conscience smote her. She had rather neglected Garnet since they had entered the Sixth Form. During their year in V.a. they had been fast friends. As new girls together and scholarship holders, a close tie had existed between them, and they had shared in many small excitements and adventures. When Winona was chosen Games Captain, however, their interests seemed to separate. Garnet was not athletic, she cared little for hockey or cricket, and preferred to devote her surplus energies to the Literary Society or the Debating Club. Almost inevitably they had drifted apart. Winona, wrapped up in the supreme fascinations of hockey matches and gymnasium practice, had chummed with Marjorie Kemp, Bessie Kirk, and Joyce Newton, who shared her enthusiasm for games. She remembered with a pang of self-reproach that she had not walked round the playground with Garnet once this term. Winona admired fidelity, but she certainly could not pride herself upon having practiced that virtue of late.

Garnet was absent from her desk next day, but when she returned to the school on Thursday, Winona sought an opportunity, and bore her off for a private talk. Garnet was looking very pale.

"I'm dreadfully upset," she confessed. "I told you I had to see a specialist about my eyes? Well, yesterday we went to

Dunningham, to consult Sir Alfred Pollard. He says there's very serious trouble, and that if I'm not careful, I may ruin my sight altogether. He absolutely forbids any home work in the evenings."

"Forbids home work!" gasped Winona.

"Yes, utterly! Just think of it! With the examinations only six weeks off! I begged and implored, but he said I might choose between my sight and my exam. I suppose I shall have to fail!"

"Oh, Garnet!"

"Yes," continued her friend bitterly, "to fail at the very end, after all my work! And I *have* worked! When other girls have been getting all sorts of fun, I've sat in my bedroom with my books. Oh, it's too cruel!... Don't think me conceited, but I thought I might have a chance for the Seaton Scholarship. It was worth trying for! If you knew how I long to go to College! It would be so glorious to write B.A. after one's name! Besides, I must do something in life. All my sisters have chosen careers, and I had, quite decided to take up teaching as a profession. I talked it over with Miss Goodson one day. She was so nice about it, and strongly advised me to go to College if I could possibly get the opportunity. Well, I suppose that dream's over now! Not much chance of a scholarship with one's prep knocked off!"

"Oh, Garnet, I'm so sorry! Will the doctor let you take the exams, at all?"

"Yes, I may attend school as usual, and go in for the exam., but I'm not to look at a book after 4 p.m. or before 9 a.m., so it's a very empty permission. How I shall rage all the evenings! I wish I had a gramophone to howl out my work into my ears, as I mayn't use my eyes!"

"Would that help you?" asked Winona eagerly.

"Of course it would! It isn't my brain that's wrong, only my eyes. I asked my cousin to read my prep. to me one evening, but it was beyond her, and we only got into a muddle. Oh dear, I could cry! To have worked to within six weeks of the exam., and then to have to slack like this! I'm the unluckiest girl in the world!"

Winona comforted her poor friend as best she could. She had an idea at the back of her mind, but she did not venture to confide it to Garnet until she had first consulted Aunt Harriet about it. It was no less a proposal than that they should do their preparation together, and that by reading the work aloud she could act eyes for her chum. It. would be difficult, no doubt, but not an utter impossibility, and it was absolutely the only way in which Garnet could receive help. It would necessitate their spending many hours daily in each other's company, and to arrange this seemed to be the difficulty. She explained the situation to Miss Beach, with some diffidence and hesitation. She was terribly afraid of receiving a snubbing, and being told that her own work was more than sufficient for her, without taking up her friend's burdens. To her surprise, however, Aunt Harriet proved sympathetic, and heartily acquiesced in the scheme. She indeed made the very kind proposal that for the six weeks until the exam. Garnet should sleep with Winona at Abbey Close, so that they might have both the evening and early morning preparation together.

Winona carried her friend to a quiet corner of the gymnasium to communicate her thrilling news.

"Win! You don't really mean it? Oh, you're big! I didn't think any one in the world would have done that for me. Do you realize what you're undertaking? It's the one thing that can save me! And only a girl who's in my own Form, and going in for the exams. herself, could do it. Nobody else understands exactly what one wants. Win! I'm ready to worship you!"

"Will your cousin let you come to stay with us?"

"I've no fear of that. She'll be as grateful to you as I am!"

Without any further loss of time, Garnet was installed at Abbey Close, and the friends began their joint preparation. Garnet, by the doctor's orders, sat with a black silk handkerchief tied over her eyes, so as to give them all the rest which was possible. Her brain was very alert, however, and her excellent memory retained most of what Winona read to her. At first there were many difficulties to be overcome, for each had had her own way of studying, but after a while they grew used to their united method, and began to make headway with the work. They thoroughly enjoyed being together. To Winona it was almost like being back at the hostel to have a companion in her bedroom, and her many jokes and bits of fun kept up Garnet's spirits. They set their alarm clock for 5.30, and began study promptly at six each morning, after eating the bread and butter and drinking the glasses of milk which, by Aunt Harriet's orders, were always placed in readiness for them. These early hours, when the day was cool, and a fresh breeze blew in through the open window, seemed the most valuable of all; their brains felt clearer, and they were often able to grasp problems and difficult points which had eluded them the evening before.

Except for the ordinary practices which formed part of the school curriculum, Winona was obliged for the present to appoint Bessie Kirk as her deputy-Captain. She had no time herself to train juniors, to act referee, or to stand watching tennis sets. It meant a great sacrifice to relinquish these most congenial duties, but she knew Miss Bishop and Miss Goodson approved, and she promised herself to return to them all the more heartily when the examination should be over. She would ask Bessie wistfully for reports of the progress of various stars who were in training, and managed to keep in touch with the games, though she could not always participate in them.

"Wait till June's over, and I'm emancipated! Then won't I have the time of my life!" she announced. "Thank goodness the match with Binworth isn't till July 21st!"

Angela Brazil

The weeks of strenuous work passed slowly by. The weather was warm and sultry, with frequent thunderstorms, not a favorable atmosphere for study. Garnet flagged palpably, and lost her roses. To Winona the time seemed interminable. The task she had undertaken of helping her friend was a formidable one. It needed all her courage to persevere. Sometimes she longed just for an evening to throw it up, and go and play tennis instead, but every hour was important to Garnet, and must not be lost. Winona often had to set her teeth and force herself to resist the alluring sound of the tennis in the next-door garden, where she had a standing invitation to come and play, and it took all the will power of which she was capable to focus her attention on the examination subjects. She tried not to let Garnet see how much the effort cost her; the latter was sensitive, and painfully conscious of being a burden. Miss Beach dosed both the girls with tonics, and insisted upon their taking a certain amount of exercise.

"Work by all means, but don't over-work," was her recommendation. "There's such a thing as bending a bow until it breaks. I don't like to see such white cheeks!"

The examination was for entering Dunningham University, and must be taken at that city. The Governors of the Seaton High School had offered a scholarship, tenable for three years, to whichever of their candidates, obtaining First Class honors, appeared highest on the list of passes. They had arranged with the examiners to place the names of the successful candidates in order of merit and on the receipt of the results they would award their exhibition. If no one obtained First Class honors, the offer would be withdrawn, and held over until another year.

Several of the girls were well up in their work, and seemed likely to have a chance of winning. Linda Fletcher had the advantage of two years in the Sixth, Agatha James was undoubtedly clever, and Beatrice Howell, though not brilliant, possessed a steady capacity for grind. With three such formidable rivals Garnet's heart might very reasonably fail her.

The doctor's prohibition was a most serious handicap for invaluable as her chum's help proved, it was not so effective as being able to use her own eyes. Sometimes she lost courage altogether, and it needed Winona's most dogged determination to keep her mind fixed unwaveringly upon the end in view.

"It's like playing in a match," Winona assured her. "If you think the other side's going to win, you may as well throw up the sponge at once. Don't give way an inch until you absolutely know you're beaten. I'm just determined you're to have that scholarship!"

"If I could only think so!" sighed Garnet. "Oh, Win! what should I do without you? When I'm with you my spirits go up, and I've courage enough for anything, and when I'm by myself I feel a wretched jelly-fish of a creature, just inclined to sit in a corner and blub!"

"No blubbering, please! Worst thing possible for the eyes!" commanded Winona.

"Well, I won't! You've cheered me up tremendously. I'm glad you'll be in the exam. room with me. I shall feel twice as brave if I know you're there!"

The days sped on, and the very last one came. Miss Bishop and Miss Goodson had given their final coachings and their most valuable help. Winona and Garnet devoted the evening to mastering one or two doubtful points.

"We've done our best, and it depends now whether we've luck in the questions," said Winona. "I think we'd better put the books away. We shall only muddle ourselves if we try any more to-night. Aunt Harriet says we're not to get up at five to-morrow. We shall have quite a hard enough day as it is."

"It wouldn't be much use," said Garnet, thrusting back the hair from her hot forehead. "I feel I've taken in the utmost my brains can hold. There's no room for anything more. How close the air is!"

"I believe we're going to have another storm," replied Winona, leaning out of the widely opened window, to gaze at the lurid sky. "There's a feeling of electricity about. Ah! There it begins!"

A vivid flash behind the tower of the old Minster was followed by a long rumble of thunder. The atmosphere was painfully oppressive. Again a white streak ran like a corkscrew over the clouds, and a louder peal resounded. The storm was drawing nearer.

"Come from the window, Winona. It's not safe!"

Garnet was terribly afraid of thunder. The electricity in the air has a powerful effect upon some temperaments, and at the first sound of heaven's artillery she was crouching beside her bed, with her head buried in the pillow.

"Don't be a silly ostrich!" retorted her chum. "It's quite far away yet, and if it does come, the chances are a thousand to one against it hitting this particular house. Why, you weren't half so scared of Zeppelins! For goodness' sake don't get hysterical! Show some pluck!"

Winona's remarks might not be complimentary, but they were bracing. Garnet laughed nervously, and consented to sit upon a chair. In about half-an-hour the storm blew over, leaving a clear sky and stars.

"Come and put your head out of the window, and feel how deliciously fresh and cool it is!" commanded Winona. "Look at that bright planet! I think it must be Jupiter. I take it as a good omen for to-morrow. The storm will have cleared your brain, and your star's in the ascendant. Here's luck to the exam.!"

The city of Dunningham was about thirty miles away from

Seaton. It was a big manufacturing city, with a highly flourishing modern university, which had lately come much to the fore, and had begun to make itself a reputation. The three days' examination was to be held in the University buildings, and all candidates were bound to present themselves there. Miss Bishop had decided that the contingent of twelve from the Seaton High School should travel to Dunningham each morning by the early express, under the charge of Miss Lever, who would take them out for lunch, and escort them safely back to Seaton again in the evening. The arrangement necessitated an early start, but nobody minded that.

The little party met at the railway station in quite bright spirits. It was rather fun, all going to Dunningham together, and having a special compartment engaged for them on the train. It was a difficult matter for thirteen people to cram into seats only intended for the accommodation of ten, but they preferred over-crowding to separation, and cheerfully took it in turns to sit on one another's knees.

"It's more like a beanfeast than the exam.!" laughed Mary Payne, handing round a packet of chocolates. "I feel I absolutely don't care!"

"I feel like a criminal on the road to execution!" groaned Helena Maitland. "Usedn't they to give the poor wretches anything they asked for? Oh, yes, thanks! I'll have a chocolate by all means, but it's crowning the victim with a garland of roses!"

"Rather mixed metaphors, my child! If you don't express yourself more clearly in your papers, I'm afraid you won't satisfy the examiners!"

"I wonder who corrects the papers?" asked Freda Long.

"Oh! some snarling old dry-as-dust, probably, who's anxious to get through the job as quickly as he can. It must be a withering experience to go through thousands of papers. Enough to

Angela Brazil

pulverize your brains for the rest of your life!"

"I don't mind the examiners' brains. It's my own I'm anxious about. If they'll last me out these three days, I'll be content to exist at a very low mental level afterwards!"

"Right you are! Ditto this child! I'm going to read nothing but the trashiest novels during the holidays!" announced Mary aggressively.

"And I'm not going to read at all! I shall just lounge and play tennis," added Hilda.

"Poor dears! I used to feel like that, but one gets over it!" smiled Miss Lever. "Don't eat too many caramels, or you'll be so thirsty in the exam room. Malted milk tablets are the best thing; they're sweet, but sustaining. Plain chocolate is the next best. I shall think of you all the whole morning."

"You'll have a lovely time gallivanting round Dunningham and shop-gazing, while we're racking our brains!" said Garnet. "We're all envious!"

"Remember, I've had my purgatory before!" returned Miss Lever, laughing. "You must allow me a good time in my old age!"

Arrived at Dunningham station, they took the tramcar, and proceeded straight to the University. It was a very fine modern building, erected round three sides of a large quadrangle, the fourth side being occupied by a museum. They were directed to the Women Students' Department, and took off their hats and coats in the dressing-room. Miss Lever, who had herself graduated at Dunningham, knew the place well, and was able to give them exact directions. She escorted them across the quadrangle to the big hall where the examination was to be held.

"The place has a classic look," said Garnet, gazing at the

Corinthian columns of the portico. "I'm afraid they won't consider my Latin up to standard. May the fates send me an easy paper!"

"You should have asked them before!" giggled Winona. "The papers are printed now, and not all the gods of Olympus could alter a letter. I accept my fortunes in the spirit of a Mahomedan. It's Kismet!"

The first set of questions was easier than the girls had dared to expect. They scribbled away eagerly. It was encouraging, at any rate, to make a good beginning. They compared notes at the end of the morning, and arrived at the conclusion that all had done fairly well. Miss Lever was waiting for them in the quadrangle when they came out, and announced that she had engaged a special table for the party at a restaurant, and had ordered a particularly nice little lunch, with coffee afterwards to clear their brains. Some of the girls were tired, and inclined to groan, others were exhilarated, but the enthusiasts cheered up the weaker spirits, and by the time the coffee course was reached, everybody was feeling courageous.

"Should I dare to suggest ices?" murmured Winona.

"All right, if you like. There's just time," assented Miss Lever, consulting her watch. "I passed my Intermediate on ices during a spell of intensely hot weather. I can allow you exactly five minutes, so choose quickly - strawberry or vanilla?"

The three days of the examination seemed to Winona like a dream. She grew quite accustomed to the big hall full of candidates, and to her particular desk. Garnet sat at the other side of the aisle, and Winona would sometimes pause a moment to watch her. To judge from her friend's absorbed appearance and fast moving pen, the papers appeared to suit her. To Winona's immense astonishment she herself was doing quite moderately well. The six weeks' coaching of Garnet had been of inestimable benefit to her own work. She had not then thought of this aspect of the matter, but she was certainly now reaping the reward of her labor of love. For the first time the possibility of gaining a pass occurred to her.

"If I do, it'll be the limit!" she reflected. "Miss Bishop will have about the surprise of her life!"

On the whole the girls quite enjoyed their three days at Dunningham. There were intervals between their various papers, which they spent partly in the University museum and partly in the City Art Gallery, where a fine collection of Old Masters was on loan. It was the first time Winona had seen paintings by world-famous artists, though she had often pored over reproductions of their works in *The Studio* or *The Connoisseur*. She felt that the experience added another window to her outlook on life.

"I wish I'd the talent to be an artist!" she thought. "There are so many things I'd like to do! Oh, dear! Painting and music (both beyond me utterly) and physical culture and poultry farming, and Red Cross nursing, and I probably shan't do any of them, after all! I want to be of solid use to the world in a nice interesting way to myself, and I expect I'll just have to do a lot of stupid things that I hate. Why wasn't I born a Raphael?"

"How do you think you've got on altogether?" Garnet asked Winona, as, thoroughly tired out, the two girls traveled homeward to Seaton at the end of the third day's examination.

"Um - tolerably. Better, perhaps, than I expected, but that's not saying much. And you?"

"I never prophesy till I know!"

But Garnet's dark eyes shone as she leaned back in her corner.

CHAPTER XIX

THE SWIMMING CONTEST

Once the examinations were over, Winona's spirits, which had been decidedly at Il Penseroso, went up to L'Allegro. The strain of coaching Garnet had been very great, but the relief was in corresponding proportion. She felt as if a burden had rolled from her shoulders. There was just a month of the term left. The Sixth would of course be expected to do its ordinary form work, but the amount of home study required would be reasonable, quite a different matter from the intolerable grind of preparation for a University examination. The extra afternoon classes with Miss Goodson were no longer necessary, leaving a delightful period of leisure half-hours at school. Winona intended to employ these blissful intervals in cricket practice, at the tennis courts, in helping to arrange the museum, and in carrying out several other pet schemes that she had been forced hitherto to set aside. Bessie Kirk had made a good deputy, but it was nice to take the reins into her own hands once more, and feel that she was head of the Games department. She coached her champions assiduously. At tennis Emily Cooper and Bertha March stood out like planets among the stars. They had already beaten Westwood High School and Hill Top Secondary School, and hoped to have a chance against Binworth College, of hitherto invincible reputation. The match would not take place for a fortnight, which gave extra time for practice. In cricket, Betty Carlisle had come to the front at bowling, while Maggie Allesley and Irene Swinburne were heroines of the bat. It is inevitable that some

Angela Brazil

girls should overtop the rest, but Winona would not on that account allow the others to slack. She knew the importance of a high general average of play, and urged on several laggers. She thoroughly realized the importance of fielding, and made her eleven concentrate their minds upon it.

"We lost Tamley on fielding," she affirmed, "and if we've any intention of beating Binworth, we've just got to practice catching and throwing in."

Of the two matches in which the school had so far taken part, the first, with Baddeley High School, had been a draw, and in the second, with Tamley, they had been beaten. It was not an encouraging record, and Winona felt that for the credit of the school it was absolutely necessary to vanquish Binworth. Its team had a fairly good reputation, so it would be no easy task, but after the hockey successes of last winter she did not despair. Apart from school she had a very pleasant time. Nearly every evening after supper Aunt Harriet would suggest a short run in the car before sunset. She generally allowed her niece to take the wheel as soon as they were clear of the town traffic, and Winona soon became quite expert at driving. She liked to feel the little car answering to her guidance; there was a thrill in rounding corners and steering past carts, and every time she went out she gained fresh confidence. She was not at all nervous, and kept her head admirably in several small emergencies, managing so well that Aunt Harriet finally allowed her to bring the car back down the High Street, which, as it was the most crowded portion of the town, was considered the motorist's ordeal in Seaton. She acquitted herself with great credit, passed a tramcar successfully, and understood the signals of the policeman who waved his hand at the corner. Aunt Harriet had taken out a driver's license for her, so having proved her skill in the High Street, she now felt quite a full-fledged lady chauffeur.

Winona immensely enjoyed these evening runs when the sky was aflame with sunset, and the trees were quiet dark masses of color, and the long road stretched out before her, pink from the glow above, and the lacey hemlocks and meadowsweets made a soft blurred border below the hedgerows. With an open road in front of her she was tempted sometimes to put on speed, and felt as if she were flying onwards into a dream country where all was vague and mysterious and shadowy and unknown. She was always loth to return, but Aunt Harriet was extremely particular that they must be home before lighting-up time, and would point remorselessly to the small clock that hung facing the seat. Perhaps Winona's greatest triumph was when, one evening, she managed without any assistance to run the car into its own shed in the garage, a delicate little piece of steering which required fine calculation, a quick hand, and a rapid turn. She was learning something of the mechanism, too, could refill the petrol tank, and was almost anxious for a tire to burst, so that she might have the opportunity of putting on the Stepney wheel, though this latter ambition was not shared by her aunt.

"When all the men have gone to the war, I'll be able to drive a taxi or a war van, and make myself useful to the Government! I believe I could clean the car perfectly well if Sam should be called up, and has to leave the garage. I'd just enjoy turning the hose on it. What would they give me a week to take Sam's place here?"

"They'd give you a snubbing if you asked them!" laughed Aunt Harriet. "Cleaning a car is uncommonly hard work. You might manage our small one, but by the time you'd done the whole round of the garage, you'd be ready to declare it wasn't a woman's job."

"I'd chance it!" retorted Winona.

She had her opportunity after all, for the garage attendant was taken ill, and remained off duty for several days. On the Saturday morning Winona set to work and cleaned, polished and oiled the car thoroughly. It was very dirty after a muddy day's use, so she had her full experience. It was certainly far harder than she had anticipated, and she felt devoutly thankful

Angela Brazil

that she was not bound to attack the cars in the other sheds, and perform similar services for each.

"Sam earns his money," she assured Aunt Harriet, when she returned at lunch-time. "On the whole, I've decided I won't be a lady chauffeur. It's bad enough to have to clean one's bicycle, but if I had to go through this car performance every day, I don't think there'd be very much left of me."

"Ah! I told you so!" returned, Aunt Harriet triumphantly.

Motoring was not the only fresh form of activity which Winona had taken up this summer. The school had organized swimming classes, and on certain clean-water days detachments of girls were conducted to the public baths. Owing to her college entrance examinations, Winona had not been able to attend the full course, but she had learnt to swim last summer at the baths, and was as enthusiastic as anybody. Miss Medland, the teacher, was an expert from Dunningham; she was skillful herself, and clever at training her pupils. The girls soon gained confidence in the water, and began to be able to perform what they called "mermaid high jinks."

The Public Baths at Seaton were most remarkably good, so good indeed that many of the citizens had raised a protest against the Corporation for spending so much money upon them. The High School girls, who had not to pay the rates, did not sympathize with the grumbles of ratepayers, and rejoiced exceedingly in the sumptuous accommodation. They specially appreciated the comfort of the dressing-rooms, and the convenience of the hot-air apparatus for drying their hair. The restaurant, where tea or bovril could be had, was also a luxury for those who were apt to turn shivery after coming from the water.

"I can understand why the Romans were so enthusiastic about their public baths," said Audrey Redfern. "Just think of having little trays of eatables floating about on the water, so that you could have a snack whenever you wanted, and slaves to bring you delicious scent afterwards, and garlands of flowers. I wish I'd lived some time B.C. instead of in the twentieth century!"

"Be thankful you didn't live in the twelfth, for then you mightn't have had a bath at all!" returned Winona; "certainly not a public one, and probably not the private one either. An occasional canful of water would have been thought quite sufficient for you, with perhaps a dip in a stream if you could get it. The people who bathed were mostly pilgrims at Holy Wells, and they all used the same water, no matter what their diseases were."

"How disgusting! Well, on the whole I'm tolerably satisfied to belong to the poor old twentieth century. It might be better, but it might be worse."

"How kind of you! I'm sure posterity will be grateful for your approval."

"D'you want me to push you into the water, Winona Woodward? I will, in half a second!"

At the end of the course it was arranged that a swimming contest should take place among the girls, and that various prizes should be offered for championships. It was the first event of the kind in the annals of the school, so naturally it aroused much enthusiasm. About thirty candidates were selected by Miss Medland as eligible for competitions, the rest of her pupils having to content themselves with looking on. A special afternoon was given up to the display, and invitations were sent out to parents to come and help to swell the audience.

"Are you in for the mermaidens' fete?" Winona asked Marjorie Kemp.

"Mermaidens' fete, indeed! How romantic we are all of a sudden! The frog fight, I should call it."

"There speaks the voice of envy! You're evidently out of it."

"Don't want to be in it, thanks! It'll be wretched work shivering round the edge of the bath for a solid hour!"

"Sour grapes, my child!" teased Winona.

"Go on, my good girl - if you want to make me raggy, you just shan't succeed, that's all!"

"Now I *should* like to have been chosen!" mourned Evelyn Richards. "I don't mind confessing that I've had a disappointment. I thought I could swim quite as well as Freda, and it's grizzly hard luck that she was picked out and I wasn't. Rank favoritism, I call it!"

"Poor old Eve! Look here, I'll tell you a secret. You head the reserve list. I know because I saw it. If anybody has a cold on the day of the event, you'll take her place."

"You mascot! Shall I? Oh! I do hope somebody'll catch cold - not badly, but just enough to make it unsafe to go into the water. You can't think how I want to try my luck. I don't suppose I've a chance of a prize, but if I did get one, why I'd cock-a-doodle-do the school down!"

"I'm quite sure you would! Trust you to blow your own trumpet!"

"Winona Woodward, if you'd been properly and thoroughly spanked in your babyhood, you'd be a much more civil person now. I decline your company. Ta-ta!"

"Poor old Eve! Take it sporting!" said Winona soothingly.

On the afternoon of the great event, the ladies' large bath was specially reserved for the school. A goodly crowd of spectators filled almost to overflowing the galleries that ran round the hall; interested fathers and mothers, sympathetic aunts, and a sprinkling of cousins and friends made up the visitors' list, and the rest of the space was crammed with school girls. Each likely champion had her own set of supporters, who murmured her name as a kind of war cry, and were only restrained from shouting it at the pitch of their lungs by the sight of Miss Bishop, who stood below, talking to Miss Medland and the judge. The enthusiasm went perhaps more by favor than by actual prowess, and could hardly be taken as an augury of success, for Barbara Jones, who was popular, received much more encouragement than Olga Dickinson, who had distanced her every time at the practices. Juniors will be juniors, however, and the fourth and third forms stamped solidly for Barbara, ignoring the superior claims of her rival.

The bath, with its blue and white tiles, looked tempting. All the school envied the candidates as they came marching in in their costumes.

"Evelyn's got a place after all!" said Garnet, who was among the spectators, to Gladys Cooper, who sat next to her. "Some one else must be off, then. Who is it? Freda Long? Poor old Freda! Got toothache? It's hard luck on her! There's Winona. I don't believe she'll win, but I'll cheer her! Rather!"

Winona also did not think it likely that she would win. She had only had time for half the lessons, which put her at a serious disadvantage with girls who had taken the full course. It was unsporting, however, to go in confident of defeat, so she meant to do her best.

The first event was the Upper School Championship for the fastest swimmer. The candidates stood ready at the edge of the bath, then at the given signal they flung themselves into the water, and started. At first they were fairly even, but after a dozen yards or so several shot ahead. The irrepressible juniors lost all control in their excitement, and cheered on each as she appeared to be gaining.

"Audrey Redfern!"

Angela Brazil

"No, no! Jess Gardner!"

"Winona Woodward!"

"Elsie Parton's passed her!"

"No, no! Winona's making up!"

"She'll never do it, though!"

"It's a draw!"

As a matter of fact Winona and Elsie Parton touched the winning tape at the very identical moment. It was a great surprise for both of them. Winona had expected Jess or Audrey to be first, and never thought of Elsie as a possible champion. Elsie was in V.b. and had not been very long at the school. No one had taken much notice of her up to now, and the girls were rather staggered at her success. They did not even clap her as she climbed up from the bath. The judge wrote down the result, and called the next event. This was the Lower School Championship, and the juniors were soon screaming for Barbara Jones and Daisy James. The latter had it by a length, and walked away smiling, to be wrapped up in a towel by Miss Lever, for she was a chilly little creature, and apt to be taken with fits of shivers if she stood long out of the water.

Diving followed, both from the edge of the bath and from the diving board. In the Senior division Audrey and Jess secured the highest scores, neither Winona nor Elsie coming near them. Winona was not really very fond of diving, while Elsie staked her all upon extreme speed. The Juniors did almost better than their elders, Olga Dickinson's achievement quite carrying the enthusiasm of the hall.

The next competition was for style. The candidates swam first on their sides, then on their backs, and finally on their backs moving their legs only, their arms being placed on their hips. The judge put down marks for each according to what she considered their deserts; until the list should be made up, nobody knew who, in her expert opinion, had done the best.

It was now the turn of the Midnight Race, a most important event, to which the spectators were looking forward keenly. Only the best swimmers were allowed to take part, the other candidates had to content themselves with watching. The selected ten retired to the dressing-room, and in a few moments emerged, each clad in a long white nightdress, and holding a candlestick with a lighted candle in her hand. A roar of applause rose from the gallery as the white-robed figures formed into line. Every girl placed her candlestick on the edge of the bath, and getting into the water, held on to the rail at attention. When the judge gave the signal, each seized her candlestick and commenced to swim on her back to the other side of the bath, holding up the candle in her left hand. It was a feat that required steadiness and skill. Evelyn Richards tried to hurry too fast, and the draft caused by her over-quick passage blew out her flame. Mollie Hill caught her foot in her nightdress, and dropped her candle altogether. Jess Gardner pursued the original method of holding her candlestick in her teeth, and using both arms to swim. There was keen excitement as the candidates cautiously worked their way across. Each was required to place her candle for a second on the edge of the bath, and then to swim back to the original starting point. Only five competitors were in the running for the return journey - Winona, Audrey Redfern, Elsie Parton, Dora Lloyd (a Fourth Form girl), and little Olga Dickinson. The temptation to swim too fast was overwhelming, and Audrey fell a victim to it, her flame going out just in the middle of the bath. Olga Dickinson actually reached the starting point the first, but Winona and Elsie Parton were only a second behind her, placing their candlesticks down at the very same moment.

"I wonder how the score's going?" said Winona, as the Seniors stood watching the Junior Handicap Race.

"I've no idea," returned Audrey. "You see we don't know what

Angela Brazil

marks Miss Gatehead has given for style, and several other things. She doesn't judge exactly like Miss Medland does. It's a pity Freda Long's out of it."

"What happened to Freda?"

"Got toothache. Can't you see her sitting up there in the gallery, holding her cheek? She's looking at you!"

"Poor old Freda! Beastly hard luck!" murmured Winona, waving a sympathetic greeting to her friend.

The Midnight Race had been intensely interesting, but the Obstacle Race proved an even greater excitement. Two thin planks of wood were placed across the bath, floating upon the water. The competitors started from the deep end, dived under the first plank, and then scrambled over the second. At the shallow end were a number of large round wash-tubs; each candidate had to seize upon one of these and seat herself in it, a most difficult feat of fine balancing, for unless she hit upon the exact center of gravity, the tub promptly overturned, and flung her into the water. It was a most mirth-provoking competition, candidates and spectators bursting into shouts of laughter as one after another the girls gingerly climbed into their tubs, and toppled over into the bath. Those who managed at last to preserve their equilibrium were given paddles, and had to navigate themselves to the nearest plank, where they invariably fell out, and were rescued and towed back by attendant nymphs told off for the purpose. Nobody succeeded in paddling to the plank and back again, and the competition resolved itself into a series of splashes, squeals and bursts of mirth. Even stately Miss Bishop was laughing heartily, and the girls in the gallery were in a state bordering on hysteria.

At last Miss Gatehead called order, and the dripping candidates retired from their water carnival to await the judging. The scores were rapidly added up, and the result was announced.

"Winona Woodward and Elsie Parton equal. They will therefore swim the length of the bath to decide the championship."

Planks and tubs were hastily cleared away from the field of action, and the rival candidates started on their final contest. The sympathies of the gallery went strongly with Winona; the girls wanted their Games Captain to win, and they cheered her vigorously. But Winona was tired, Elsie Parton was lithe and active, and had made fast swimming her specialty. Winona did her sporting best, but by the middle of the bath Elsie had distanced her, and reached the winning post a whole length ahead.

There was dead silence from the girls in the gallery. Their Captain had failed, and they did not mean to applaud her opponent. Winona, looking upwards, saw the popular feeling in their faces. All her generous spirit rose in revolt. She was standing close to Miss Bishop, Miss Gatehead and Miss Medland, and therefore it was certainly a breach of school etiquette for her to do what she did, but acting on the impulse of the moment she shouted: "Cheer, you slackers! Three cheers for Elsie Parton!" and waving her hand as a signal, led off the "Hip-hip-hip hurrah!" A very volume of sound followed, and the roof rang as Miss Bishop presented the winner with the cup for the Championship.

"Thanks *awfully*, Winona!" said Elsie, as the girls walked away to the dressing-rooms. "I'm afraid I've disappointed the school - but I did want to win!"

"Of course you did - and why shouldn't you? I hope I can take a beating in a sporting way! I think I made them ashamed of themselves. Fair play and no favoritism is the tradition of this school, and I mean to have no nasty cliquey feeling in it so long as I'm Games Captain, or my name's not Winona Woodward! That's the law of the Medes and Persians!"

CHAPTER XX

THE RED CROSS HOSPITAL

Winona received constant letters from Percy in the trenches "somewhere in France," all, of course, carefully censored. They had arranged a cryptogram before he left England, however, and by its aid he was able to tell her the name of the place near which he was fighting. It was a tremendous excitement for her when his letters arrived to fetch her key to the cryptogram and reckon out the magic little word that let her know his whereabouts. She would find the spot on the big war-map that hung in the dining-room and would mark it with a miniature flag, feeling in closer touch with him now she knew exactly where he was located. She kept a special album in which she placed photos of him in khaki, all his letters and postcards, and any newspaper cuttings that concerned his regiment. The book was already half full; she looked it over almost daily, and kept it as, at present, her greatest treasure.

She sent parcels regularly to Percy. Campaigning had not destroyed his boyish love for sweetstuff, and he welcomed cakes, toffee and chocolate. "I share it with the other chaps," he wrote, "and they give you a vote of thanks every time. You wouldn't believe what larks we have in our dug-out!"

Percy's letters were in his old gay style, but every now and then Winona noticed a more serious vein running through them. He had sad news to tell sometimes. Two of his special chums were killed in action, the young doctor was shot while attending to the wounded, and their chaplain had been injured. "We never know when our turn will come," he finished, and Winona shivered as she kissed the letter and put it away.

She looked up sometimes at the calm clear globe of the full moon and thought how it was shining down alike on the far-away trenches of France and the great Minster towers of Seaton. How many battles had it seen in the earth's history, and how many still forms lying stiff and straight under its pale beams? Men fought and died, and the moon and the stars passed on their way, uncaring - but God cared, and at the back of it all His Hand was guiding the world, and even from seeming chaos would bring good out of evil at His own time. "God bless Percy, and bring him safe home!" prayed Winona passionately, but she felt in her heart of hearts that if the Great Captain called him, she could bend her head in the knowledge that He knew best.

With the hot July weather Aunt Harriet's health flagged. She seemed suddenly to have grown much older. The erect figure stooped a little, her high color had faded and her voice lost some of its energy and determination. She was not able to fulfill all her former public duties, and she fretted greatly at the enforced inaction. She was one of those characters who would rather wear out than rust out, and it required the utmost firmness on the part of her doctor to persuade her from over-exerting herself. Instead of being in a continual whirl of creche committee meetings, workhouse inspections, and creche management, she now spent long quiet afternoons in the shaded drawing-room learning that (to her) hardest of all lessons, how to rest! Winona, busy with the last exciting weeks of the school term, was too occupied to give much thought to her aunt, but could not help remarking that the latter's spirits had failed lately. Miss Beach was far gentler than of yore. She did not snap her niece up so suddenly, or give vent to excited tirades about subjects which irritated her. Sometimes she even looked at Winona with a wistfulness that the girl noticed. It puzzled her, for it was the same half-appealing glance that her

Angela Brazil

mother often cast at her. She was accustomed to shoulder her mother's burdens, and loved her all the more for her helplessness and dependence. But Aunt Harriet, so strong and determined and capable, the oracle of the family, and the very epitome of all the cardinal virtues, surely *she* could not want any one to lean upon? The idea was unthinkable. Yet again and again it returned to her, and the consciousness of it stirred new chords.

One evening Winona came rather softly into the drawing-room. Her aunt, sitting by the window in the gathering twilight, did not hear her enter. Miss Beach was reading, and the last little gleam of the sunset fell on her gray hair. How worn she looked, Winona thought. It had never struck her so forcibly before. Was that a tear shining on her cheek? Miss Beach rose slowly, put down her book, took her handkerchief from her bag and deliberately wiped her eyes; then, still unconscious of her niece's presence, she went out through the French window into the garden.

Winona walked across the room, hesitated for a moment but did not venture to follow her. Almost automatically she took up the book which Aunt Harriet had been reading. It was a little volume of extracts, and one had been marked with a penciled cross: -

"Put your arms around me -
There, like that:
I want a little petting
At life's setting,
For 'tis harder to be brave
When feeble age comes creeping,
And finds me weeping,
Dear ones gone.
Just a little petting
At life's setting:
For I'm old, alone and tired,
And my long life's work is done."

The tears rushed to Winona's eyes. Did Aunt Harriet really feel like that? Oh, why could she not go and comfort her? She turned impulsively into the garden. The slow steps were coming back up the paved walk. She would have given worlds to walk up to her aunt and fling her arms round her, but the old sense of shyness and reserve held her back. Miss Beach was passing along the border, her dress brushing the flowers as she went by. It would surely be easy to join her, and at least to take her arm! Easy? No! She had never done such a thing in her life with her aunt. A peck of a kiss was the only mark of affection that they had hitherto exchanged. Winona looked and longed to express her sympathy, but the invisible barrier seemed strong as ever. Aunt Harriet turned aside and went towards the kitchen. The opportunity was lost.

"How horribly we live right inside ourselves!" thought Winona. "How few people know just what we're feeling and thinking, and how hard it is to let them know! The 'I' at the back of me is so different from the outside of me! When I want to say things I turn stupid and my tongue stops. I suppose most other people feel really the same, and we all live in our own little world and only touch one another now and then. Human speech is such a poor medium. Will it be dropped in the next life, and shall we talk with our hearts?"

It was on the very morning after this that Winona received an agitated letter from home. Her mother had bad news. Percy had been wounded, and was in the Red Cross Hospital at Prestwick. Mrs. Woodward wrote hurriedly, for she was on the point of starting off to see him, but she promised to send a bulletin directly after her visit. Winona spent a horrible day. Percy was never for a moment out of her thoughts. The insufficiency of the information made it harder to bear. She did not know whether the wound was slight or dangerous, and her fears whispered the worst. The next report, however, was more reassuring. Percy had had an operation and the doctors hoped that with care he ought to do well. A daily bulletin would be sent to his mother, and she promised to forward it punctually to Abbey Close.

"But I shan't get it till the day afterwards!" exclaimed Winona tragically. "Oh, how I wish he were at the Red Cross Hospital here instead of at Prestwick! If I could only see him!"

"Cheer up! Things might be worse!" remarked her aunt briefly.

Miss Beach said no more at the moment, but at supper time she announced:

"We shall have to breakfast early to-morrow morning, Winona. You and I are going to Prestwick for the day. I've asked Miss Bishop to let you off."

"To Prestwick?" gasped Winona. "To the Red Cross Hospital? Oh, Aunt Harriet, do you suppose they'll let us see Percy?"

"It's visitors' day, for I telegraphed to inquire. I wasn't going on a wild-goose chase, I assure you. I know the red tape of hospitals only too well. We may see him between two-thirty and four o'clock. It's a long journey, of course, and the trains are awkward from Seaton, but we can be back by nine."

"Oh, thank you! Thank you!" said Winona, with shining eyes.

She lay awake for hours that night thinking of to-morrow's expedition. Her brain seemed turning round and round in a whirl. To see Percy and assure herself that he was alive, and likely to recover! Oh, it was worth traveling to the North Pole! When at last she slept her dreams were a confusion of agonized escapes from Zeppelins, or rushing from trenches pursued by Germans. She was glad to wake, even though it was much too early yet to get up. The sun was only just rising behind the Minster towers. Never mind! It was morning, and to-day, actually to-day, she would see Percy!

By nine o'clock Miss Beach and Winona were speeding along in the express for Dunningham. Here they changed, and began a slow and tiresome cross-country journey, with a couple of hours to wait at an uninteresting junction.

"We shall get back a little quicker than we came," Aunt Harriet explained, "because we can take advantage of the boat express, which will save us an hour and a half. It's most wearisome to jog along in these local trains, stopping at every tiny little station."

"One longs to be in the car," said Winona.

"We might have gone in the car if it had been within reasonable distance. We couldn't possibly have motored to Prestwick and back in a day, though! Trains may be hot and stuffy, but they get one over the ground."

It was nearly two o'clock before they reached their destination. They had just time for a hasty lunch at a restaurant, and then Aunt Harriet hailed a taxi and they drove to the hospital. This was a large, fine house in the suburbs, given up by its patriotic owner to the use of the Red Cross. As they turned in at the gate they could see an attractive garden, where groups of Tommies in their blue invalid uniforms were lounging in deck chairs, or lying full length on rugs spread upon the grass. An orderly showed them to the office, where Miss Beach had a brief interview with the Commandant, and they were then escorted by a V.A.D. nurse to the Queen Mary Ward.

Winona had not been in a hospital before, so all was new to her - the large airy room with its polished floor and wide-open windows, the rows of beds, each with its little cupboard by the side, the table full of flowers in the center, the nurses in their neat Red Cross uniforms. She had no time, however, for more than a hurried glance round; her eyes were busy searching for the one particular bed that was the object of their journey.

"Private Woodward is in Number eleven," said the V.A.D., motioning them to the right-hand side of the room.

Percy lay on his back with a cradle over his injured leg. His face was very white and thin, and greatly changed. The old boyish expression had vanished, there were firm lines round

Angela Brazil

the mouth and a resolute look in the eyes, which had not been there before. A few months in the trenches, and a baptism of fire, had transformed the careless, happy-go-lucky lad into a man. Tears glistened in Winona's eyes as she bent down to kiss him. It was hard to see her active brother lying helpless and suffering.

"Oh, I'm better now," he replied in answer to her inquiries. "I don't have pain all the time. I was pretty bad after the meds. had been doing their carving. I can tell you I welcomed the morphia! But I don't need it so often now, and my leg's going on splendidly. It'll be a first-rate job when it's finished. Old Jackson promises to have me out of bed on crutches before so long!"

"Crutches!" gasped Winona, in alarm.

"Why, just at first, of course!"

"We hope he won't need to use them for long," said Aunt Harriet. "The Commandant tells me they're very proud of your case at the hospital, Percy! They flatter themselves they've saved your leg where some surgeons would have amputated. You seem very comfortable here. It's a nice ward."

"Oh, yes, they're angelic to me. I'm a spoilt child, I can tell you. I was lucky to get into a 'Red Cross.' They're stuffing us here all day, and those chaps that can go about are having the time of their lives - motor drives, tea parties, concerts, and all the rest of it! The Prestwick people regularly fete them. One of our V.A.D.'s here has asked a dozen of us out to tea at her own home to-morrow. I wish I could go! It's the nurse who showed you in. She's ripping."

"I've always heard 'V.A.D.' stands for 'Very Attractive Damsel,'" laughed Winona.

"Don't lose your heart before you're twenty-one, Percy!" said Aunt Harriet, smiling quite indulgently. "You've two and a half years left yet!"

"When a chap's in the Army his age doesn't count!" declared Percy with dignity.

Most of the beds in the ward were empty at present, their owners being outside in the garden. Only four were occupied. Each of these Tommies had his own little group of visitors, and was too busy talking to them to take much notice of anybody else. Miss Beach spent a short time at Percy's bedside, then, thinking that the brother and sister would like to be left alone together she expressed her intention of looking over the hospital, and went to find a V.A.D. to show her round.

"It was ever so decent of Aunt Harriet to bring you, Tiddleywinks!" said Percy. "The mater said I mustn't expect you to come!"

"Aunt Harriet's a trump when you know her!"

"You used to call her a dragon."

"I don't now."

"Look here! I often wish I hadn't burnt that paper of hers. You know what I mean! I've kept thinking about it while I've been lying here. It was a blighter's trick to do, when she was paying my school fees. She ought to be told about it! I feel that now. You haven't breathed anything, have you?"

"Not a word! I promised, you remember."

"You can keep a secret, Win. I'll say that for you! Somehow I feel as if I want to make a clean breast of it. Aunt Harriet's done a lot for our family. I'd tell her now, only very likely when she comes back a nurse will be with her. It's just tea-time."

"Could you write to her?"

"A ripping idea! I never thought of that. I'll write to-morrow. I'll be glad to get it off my mind. Somehow, when one's been through all this, one feels quite differently about things."

The entrance of tea trays interrupted the conversation. Miss Beach returned in company with a nurse, and reminded her niece that if they wished to catch their train home they must be starting at once. It was hard to say good-by, but Winona went away infinitely comforted. Dearly as she had always loved the old Percy, she felt the new one whom she had met to-day had the makings of a stronger and finer character than she had ever dared to hope.

"The Commandant gives an excellent report of him," said Miss Beach as they drove away. "I asked her particularly if there were any likelihood of his remaining lame, but she says not. The surgeon declares he'll have him back in the trenches in the autumn."

"How glorious! Percy's just wild to go back. I believe he'll do something splendid, and get a commission, or perhaps win the Victoria Cross!"

Winona's face shone. She had been proud of Percy to-day.

The long journey home to Seaton was very tedious, though not quite so trying as the morning one, for they were able to catch the boat express to Lapton and have tea on the train. At Lapton Junction, however, they were obliged to change to a local line, and jog along at the rate of about thirty miles an hour in a particularly dusty compartment. It had been a hard day for Miss Beach. She looked very weary as she leaned back in her corner, so overdone indeed that Winona was afraid she was going to have one of her heart attacks. The threatened trouble passed, however, and as the evening grew cooler she seemed to revive. The trains were late, so it was nearly ten o'clock before they at last reached home.

"'Mighty pleased with our day's outing,' to quote Mr. Pepys," said Aunt Harriet. "It was worth going!"

"If it hasn't tired you too much!" Winona ventured to add.

On the following Sunday morning Miss Beach received a letter from Percy. She made no comment upon it at the time, but in the evening, after church, when she and Winona were walking in the garden in the twilight, she referred to it.

"I'm deeply touched by Percy's letter," she remarked. "I did not think the boy had such nice feeling in him. You understand, of course, what he has written to me about?"

"Oh, Aunt Harriet, has he told you?" burst out Winona. "Oh, I'm so very, very glad! I've been longing and yearning to tell you all these years, only I couldn't, because I'd promised - and - oh, I must tell you now - I asked you about your will - and you thought I was horrid and scheming - but it wasn't that at all - it was that I thought you ought to know the will wasn't there, and hoped that perhaps you'd look! Oh, please believe me that I didn't mean to hint that you should leave anything to me! I don't want anything! You've been so good to me! I owe you a thousand times more than I can ever pay back. I've always wanted to make you understand this, but somehow I couldn't. Thank you, thank you, thank you for all you've done for me! I shall be better all my life for having lived with you and known you. I'm a different person since I came to Seaton, and I owe it entirely to you!"

The barrier was down at last. For once Winona spoke straight from her heart. Miss Beach took off her pince-nez, wiped them, and put them in their case. Her hand was trembling.

"I wish I had known this before, child!" she said, with a break in her voice. "Here for nearly two years I have been thinking hard things of you, and imagining that you were plotting and scheming to get my money. You hurt me beyond expression when you asked if I had made my will. As a matter of fact the document is safe at my lawyer's. The paper which Percy destroyed was only a rough draft. I had forgotten its existence."

"But you do believe me?" urged Winona. "You know I had none of those horrible plans? Oh, dear Aunt Harriet, money is nothing, nothing! It is you yourself I love, if you'll only let me!"

And in the dusk of the garden, Winona, for the first time in her life, flung her warm young arms round her aunt and hugged her heartily.

CHAPTER XXI

THE END OF THE TERM

"Look here, my hearties!" said Winona to the cricket team. "Do you realize that Seaton *versus* Binworth is on Wednesday week? If you don't, it's time you did, and you'd better buck up! My opinion of you at this present moment is that you're a set of loafers! What are you doing lounging about here, when you ought to be practicing for all you're worth?"

The little group sitting on the grass under the lilac bushes smiled indulgently.

"Go ahead! Lay it on thick!" twittered Betty Carlisle. "We knew when you hove into sight that we might expect some jaw-wag!"

"It's all very fine to sermonize," yawned Maggie Allesley, "but you'd oblige me very much by going indoors and inspecting the thermometer in the hall."

"One can't tear about in this heat!" added Irene Swinburne.

"What a set of dainty Sybarites you are! No one would ever win matches if they waited for the right kind of day to practice. It's always too hot or too cold or too wet, or too something!"

"Well, to-day it's decidedly too something! Don't roast us!"

Angela Brazil

"But I shall roast you! D'you mean to let Binworth have a complete walk-over? I'll tell you what - if you can't or won't play during the heat, will you all come back to school for an hour every evening, and practice then? I'd square it up with Miss Bishop. I'm sure she wouldn't mind."

"There's sense in your remarks now," admitted Irene, sitting up. "I'm game, if others are!"

"And so's this child!" agreed Betty Carlise. "I can put the screw on Cassie and Nell, and bring them along any evening."

"Then mind you do! I'm going to take an oath of the whole team to meet here at seven each night. I shall write it down on a piece of paper, and make you all put your names to it, like signing the pledge."

"Right you are, O She-who-must-be-obeyed!"

"Your humble servants, Ma'am!"

Their Captain's suggestion of an evening cricket practice was welcomed by the team, and approved by Miss Bishop. It was delightfully cool at seven o'clock; the girls, instead of being languid and half-hearted, were energetic and enthusiastic, and their play became a different matter altogether. Winona, who had been decidedly down about the prospects of the match, began to feel more confidence. Betty's bowling was improving daily, and Irene, who had been given to blind swiping, was gaining discretion. If they would continue to make progress at the same rate, Seaton would have a chance.

"It would be too bad if we lost the last match of the season!" fluttered Winona. "While I'm your captain I want to break the record."

"All right, old girl! It shall be a kind of Charge of the Light Brigade. 'Theirs but to do or die!' It will probably be a broiling hot day, but we'll play till we drop!" Betty assured her.

"Only have the Ambulance Corps ready with fans and stretchers to revive us and bear us from the field!" added Irene, giggling.

"I'll see there's lemonade for you!"

Though to Winona, as Games Captain, "Seaton *v.* Binworth" seemed the one event worth living for, there were plenty of other interests going on in the school. Linda Fletcher, the head girl, was arranging a program for the Parents' Afternoon, the efficient performance of which was, in her eyes, of infinitely greater public importance than the cricket match. She also required numerous rehearsals, and the conflicting claims on the girls' time became so confusing that after one or two struggles between rival "whips," who contended hotly for possession, the chiefs were obliged to strike a bargain, Winona releasing two members of the team in order that they might act, and filling up their places from her reserve, while Linda undertook to leave the rest of the eleven out of her calculations. After this there was peace, and Violet Agnew and Averil Walmer, who had been secretly burning to distinguish themselves in the dramatic line in preference to athletics, could meet Winona with clear consciences.

Among other items of the program, Linda had fixed upon a French Pastoral Play, which was to be acted in the garden among the trees and lilac bushes. The girls were really supposed to get up the whole of the little entertainment by themselves, but Mademoiselle was kind in this instance, and helped to coach them. The scene was to be a Fete Champetre, and the costumes were to be copied from some of Watteau's pictures. There were tremendous consultations over them. A dressmaking Bee was held every afternoon from four to five o'clock in the small lecture-room, Miss Bishop generously lending her sewing machine for the purpose. Here a band of willing workers sat and stitched and chattered and laughed and ate chocolates, while pretty garments grew rapidly under their fingers. The dresses were only made of cheap materials, and were hastily put together, but they had a very good effect, for the colors were gay, and the style, with its panniers and lace frills was charming. The girls would hardly have managed the cutting out quite unaided, had not Miss Lever offered her assistance. "Dollikins" had large experience in the preparation of school theatricals, and possessed many invaluable paper patterns, so she was given a royal welcome, and installed at the table with the biggest and sharpest pair of scissors at her disposal.

On the afternoon fixed for the entertainment quite a goodly audience assembled to watch and applaud. Mothers were in the majority, with a fair number of aunts and elder sisters, and just a sprinkling of fathers. Forms had been carried into the garden and arranged as an amateur theater, a flat piece of lawn with a background of bushes serving as stage. The program was to be representative of the whole school, so the first part was devoted to the performances of the Juniors. Twelve small damsels selected from Forms I. and II. gave a classic dance. They were dressed in Greek costume with sandals, and wore chaplets of roses round their hair. They had been carefully trained by Miss Barbour, the drill mistress, and went through their parts with a joyousness reminiscent of the Golden Age. The Morris Dance which followed, rendered by members of Forms III. and IV., though hardly so graceful, was sprightly and in good time, the fantastic dresses with their bells and ribbons suiting most of their wearers. It was felt that the Juniors had distinguished themselves, and "Dollikins," who with Miss Barbour had worked hard on their behalf, felt almost justified in bragging of their achievements.

Meantime the Seniors had been making ready, and presently from behind the bushes tripped forth a charming group of Louis XV. courtiers, pattering the prettiest of French remarks. Dorrie Pollack as Monsieur le Duc de Tourville was a model of gallantry in a feathered hat and stiff ringlets (the result of an agonizing night passed in tight knobby curl papers!), while Linda, as Madame la Comtesse, quite outdid herself in the depth of her curtseys, and the distinguished grace with which she extended her hand for her cavalier to kiss. Nora Wilson tripped over her sword in her excitement, and Violet Agnew forgot her part, and had to be prompted by Mademoiselle, who stood with the book behind a bush; but these were only minor accidents, and on the whole the scene passed off with flying colors, and greatly impressed the parents and aunts with the high stage of proficiency in the French language attained by the pupils of Seaton High School.

Linda was so elated by the success of the afternoon that she sat up long after she ought to have been in bed that night, writing an account of the proceedings for the School Magazine. The manuscript, couched in antique language, was headed:

"YE SEATON CHRONICLE.

"Then whereas ye damsels at ye schule had laboured well and diligently during many days at ye tasks set them by their reverend elders, it seemed good to those that did govern to appoint unto them a day to make merry and rejoice. Therefore did they choose out certain among them, and arraying them in goodly fashion, did charge them to dance, to instruments of music before ye face of ye whole assembly of ye damsels, and likewise of some of their kindred, ye which were gathered together. Then did ye maids with no small skill tread ye dance, clad in fair garments with gauds and ornaments of silver upon them, at ye sight of which their kindred did raise cries of joy, and did further make great ado with clapping of ye hands. And when ye little maidens had duly presented their dances before ye company, then did ye elder damosels give a goodly masque, being decked forth in brave trappings, and speaking cunningly in ye tongue of ye fair lande of France, wherein all who heard them might well understand. And ye kindred and alle they that were gathered together for to look upon them did in kindness and with glad hearts commend them, and did of their charity vouchsafe to say that ye like had not aforetime been witnessed at ye schule, whereat ye maidens rejoiced greatly, as evenso it seemed unto them a reward for their diligent labour."

"We shall leave an account of our doings behind us," said Linda to some of her friends in the Sixth, "for the copies of the School Magazine are to be bound, and kept in the library for ever and a day. Future generations of girls will at least see our names and our Form photo, if they don't know anything else about us."

Winona was living for one event, the match with Binworth. This was not to take place on the playing grounds of either school, but on a very superior cricket ground hired for the occasion from a local club. Winona, as Secretary for Seaton, had made fullest arrangements, including the presence in the pavilion of a cheery little woman from a neighboring restaurant, who undertook the purveying of lemonade, ginger pop, cakes, and any fruit which might be obtainable for the occasion.

Tickets of admission to the ground were issued and distributed throughout the school, public opinion deeming attendance almost compulsory. The team were inspected and criticized beforehand almost as the Roman gladiators used to be reviewed by their patrons. Winona was on the whole proud of her eleven. Though not up to the lofty standard at which she had aimed, she felt that they realized a very respectable degree of merit.

The ground lay a few miles out of the city, and was reached as a rule by tramcar, but as the ordinary service would be utterly unable to cope with the large numbers who proposed going, special omnibuses and brakes had been put on for the occasion to accommodate the school, which turned out almost in full force to witness the show. Binworth also contributed its quota of spectators, so the stands of the cricket ground were rapidly filled.

Winona had a short preliminary talk with Dora Evans, who commanded the rival team, and as soon as the clock in the pavilion pointed to 2.30 the Captains stood out to toss.

"Heads!" cried Winona. "It's tails! Your choice!"

"We'll bat, then," decreed Dora.

Winona placed her field at once, and Dora, after a whispered word or two to her team, selected her first bats. One was a business-like looking girl who hummed a tune as she came, with ostentatious carelessness; the other, stout and dark, blinked her eyes nervously. It was manifestly impossible to judge their capacities beforehand. Betty Carlisle was to take the first over. She had a high overhand action, and sent the ball down the pitch at a good pace. Lottie Moir, the dark-haired damsel who faced the bowling, was cautious. She played the first ball respectfully back to the bowler. The next, being of good length, she played quietly to long-off for one. She was evidently not out to take risks, and the rest of the over she did not attempt to score. Her partner, Meg Perkins, was a fairly brilliant, but more reckless player. The first ball she received came down at a good pace, but well on the off-side of the wicket. A well-timed cut sent it flying to the short boundary for two. Perhaps the success turned her head a little. The next ball pitched well to the leg-side; she made a mighty stroke at it, not allowing for the break, and missed it altogether. Next moment she was walking ruefully back to the pavilion.

Phyllis Knight, the next bat, was evidently regarded by the Binworth team as a champion. She was tall, and decidedly athletic looking. Winona nodded to Irene Swinburne, celebrated for her twisters, and Irene went on to bowl. Phyllis had a long reach, which she employed successfully in driving the first ball she received right along the ground into "the country" for three. Seaton began to look rather glum. The next ball she stone-walled. Irene was growing desperate. Phyllis was waiting with her bat slightly raised. "Now if only I can drop the ball just under that bat, out she goes!" said Irene to herself, and sent the swiftest she knew how. Phyllis made a slash at it, evidently thinking it a half volley, but alas! her bails flew, and the Seaton contingent were roaring "Well bowled!"

None of the rest of the Binworth team approached to Phyllis' standard, though they played with caution, and their score mounted up steadily. At the end of their innings sixty was up on the board.

The Binworth Captain now arranged her field, and Winona sent in Bessie Kirk and Irene Swinburne to face the bowling of Meg Perkins at one end, and Phyllis Knight at the other. At first things did not go over well for Seaton. Bessie Kirk fell a victim to Meg's crafty slows. She played too soon at a short-pitched ball, and spooned a catch to mid-on. Irene at first scored merrily, but growing foolhardy was clean bowled by Phyllis Knight, to her huge discomfiture. Betty Carlisle and Maggie Allesley met with better luck, and the score began to creep up. The Seaton girls breathed more freely. Audrey Redfern and Lizzie Morris came up next. Lizzie broke her duck in the first over, and gaining confidence began to get her eye in, and with Audrey stone-walling with dogged persistence at the other end, and now and then making a single, the score reached fifty-three. There were only ten minutes left. Winona began to grow desperate. She came forth herself now, with a look of determination on her face. Dora Evans at once rolled the ball to Lottie Moir. Winona took her block composedly. Lottie might with advantage have been put on before. Her style, though by no means swift, was most awkward to play. Winona in the first over did not attempt to score. She wished to take the measure of her opponent. In the next over her partner made a single, which brought Winona to the opposite wicket. The first ball came well on the off-side, and she sent it flying to the boundary for four. Fifty-eight was now up on the board, and there were only five minutes left! Perhaps Lottie Moir was tired, or waxed a little c areless.The next ball she sent down was an easy full pitch. Winona waited till just the right moment, and then, with a fine swing of her bat, sent the ball clean over the boundary for six. The match was won, and Seaton, in the ecstasy of victory, was cheering itself hoarse.

"I never thought we'd do it!" murmured Winona to Betty, as they drank ginger pop together in the pavilion.

"I reckoned our Captain wouldn't fail us!" chuckled Betty delightedly. "Linda must compose an epic on it for the School Magazine. It beats Marathon, in my opinion!"

"Well, I'm glad my last match at the old 'High' has been a success, anyway!"

"Seaton *versus* Binworth" had taken place on Wednesday, and the school had scarcely finished exulting over its triumph before another matter claimed its attention.

On Thursday morning the results of the examination arrived. Miss Bishop summoned the whole school into the lecture hall to hear the news. She was looking flushed and excited. She waited a few moments as if to give extra effect to her words, then announced:

"I have just received the results of the Entrance Examinations from Dunningham University. Out of twelve candidates who were entered from this school, ten have satisfied the examiners. Their names stand as follows in order of merit:

FIRST CLASS.

Garnet Emerson.

SECOND CLASS.

Linda Fletcher.
Agatha James.
Helena Maitland.
Freda Long.

THIRD CLASS.

Mary Payne.
Hilda Langley.
Winona Woodward.
Dorrie Pollack.

Estelle Harrison."

Winona heaved an immense sigh of mingled amazement and relief. She had passed! Actually passed! She - Winona Woodward, whose form record had never soared above the most modest average. It was an unprecedented and altogether delightful finale to her school career. For the moment she could hardly believe that it was true. But Miss Bishop had not finished her speech; she held up her hand to stop the burst of clapping, and continued:

"As you are aware, the Governors of the School offered a three years' scholarship, tenable at Dunningham University, to whichever of the candidates should head the list, being not lower than second class. Garnet Emerson, who has secured a First Class, is therefore, at the desire of the Governors, awarded the scholarship. Now if you like to clap for her, you may do so!"

That Garnet, her dear Garnet, should have won the coveted scholarship, put the coping-stone on Winona's glee. She squeezed her friend's hand afterwards in an ecstasy of congratulation. Garnet said little, so little that her enthusiastic chum was almost disappointed. Winona, judging by her own feelings, expected her to be at delirium point. Beatrice Howell and Olave Parry, the two candidates who had failed, were receiving condolences with chastened resignation, the rest were in various stages of jubilee.

That evening, about six o'clock, a small packet was left at Abbey Close, directed to Miss Winona Woodward. She opened it eagerly. It held a small jewelers' box containing a beautiful little ring, and was accompanied by a letter from Garnet.

"DEAR WIN" (so the letter ran), - "You must have thought me slack this morning when you were congratulating me, but the fact was I was utterly overwhelmed. I'd hoped and hoped to win the scholarship, and then put the idea away, and when I knew my good fortune I just felt stunned. It's all owing to you, for if you hadn't helped me I could never, never even have passed. I don't know how to thank you. Words are quite inadequate. But will you believe that I shall never forget your kindness all the rest of my life, and will you accept this little ring and wear it for my sake? It is a garnet, and belonged to my grandmother, after whom I was named. I value it greatly, but I would far rather know you have it than keep it myself.

"Always your most grateful friend,

"GARNET EMERSON."

There was a further surprise for Winona that evening. When supper was over, and she and Miss Beach were taking their usual twilight stroll round the garden, Aunt Harriet, who had been silent for a few minutes, suddenly spoke.

"I wish to say something to you, Winona. I'm very gratified indeed to hear that you have passed your college examinations. It has given me a better opinion of your capacity and perseverance than I possessed before. This result, combined with your conduct in coaching your friend through all these weeks, has decided me in a project that I was debating in my mind. I am going to send you either to a Physical Training College to qualify as a Games Mistress, or to a Horticultural College to prepare for a National Rural Economy diploma. Whichever career you decide to choose, I am resolved that you shall have the best training available."

"Oh, Aunt Harriet! Thank you! Thank you! I don't deserve it!" faltered Winona.

The end of the term had come at length. The next day was Winona's very last at Seaton High School. She was loth to leave, for the two years she had passed there had been the happiest and the fullest in her life. But though the past had pleasant memories, the future also held out fair hopes to her.

Angela Brazil

As she entered Miss Bishop's study to say good-by, the head-mistress looked up kindly.

"I shall miss you, Winona. I have just been turning over your school record. It's not perhaps brilliant, but it has been persevering, and I am sure you've done your best. I am particularly pleased that you have passed your examination. As Games Captain you have been a decided asset to the school. I think I may safely say that you have justified the decision of the Governors in allowing you to hold the County Scholarship. Your aunt tells me that you are to go in either for Physical Training or Horticulture. Don't decide in a hurry. Get to know as much as you can about both, and think the matter over. Remember if ever you want a friend to come to me. Good-by!"

Outside in the playground the Juniors were hanging about rather shyly and awkwardly. As Winona came from the dressing-room, Daisy James, much nudged by the others, advanced and thrust a little parcel into her hand.

"It's a present from us Juniors," she said hurriedly. "Please take it! It's not much - only a birthday book - but we've all written our names in it, so that you mayn't forget us. You've been so awfully good all the year in coaching us at hockey and cricket. I don't know what we're going to do without you when you've gone! Now, girls, are you ready? One, two, three!"

And the ring of Juniors standing round shouted in one unanimous chorus: "Three cheers for our Games Captain! Hip-hip-hooray!"

Choose from Thousands of 1stWorldLibrary Classics By

A. M. Barnard	C. M. Ingleby	Elizabeth Gaskell
Ada Leverson	Carolyn Wells	Elizabeth McCracken
Adolphus William Ward	Catherine Parr Traill	Elizabeth Von Arnim
Aesop	Charles A. Eastman	Ellem Key
Agatha Christie	Charles Amory Beach	Emerson Hough
Alexander Aaronsohn	Charles Dickens	Emilie F. Carlen
Alexander Kielland	Charles Dudley Warner	Emily Dickinson
Alexandre Dumas	Charles Farrar Browne	Enid Bagnold
Alfred Gatty	Charles Ives	Enilor Macartney Lane
Alfred Ollivant	Charles Kingsley	Erasmus W. Jones
Alice Duer Miller	Charles Klein	Ernie Howard Pie
Alice Turner Curtis	Charles Hanson Towne	Ethel May Dell
Alice Dunbar	Charles Lathrop Pack	Ethel Turner
Allen Chapman	Charles Romyn Dake	Ethel Watts Mumford
Ambrose Bierce	Charles Whibley	Eugenie Foa
Amelia E. Barr	Charles Willing Beale	Eugene Wood
Amory H. Bradford	Charlotte M. Braeme	Eustace Hale Ball
Andrew Lang	Charlotte M. Yonge	Evelyn Everett-green
Andrew McFarland Davis	Charlotte Perkins Stetson	Everard Cotes
Andy Adams	Clair W. Hayes	F. H. Cheley
Anna Alice Chapin	Clarence Day Jr.	F. J. Cross
Anna Sewell	Clarence E. Mulford	F. Marion Crawford
Annie Besant	Clemence Housman	Federick Austin Ogg
Annie Hamilton Donnell	Confucius	Ferdinand Ossendowski
Annie Payson Call	Coningsby Dawson	Francis Bacon
Annie Roe Carr	Cornelis DeWitt Wilcox	Francis Darwin
Annonaymous	Cyril Burleigh	Frances Hodgson Burnett
Anton Chekhov	D. H. Lawrence	Frances Parkinson Keyes
Arnold Bennett	Daniel Defoe	Frank Gee Patchin
Arthur Conan Doyle	David Garnett	Frank Harris
Arthur M. Winfield	Dinah Craik	Frank Jewett Mather
Arthur Ransome	Don Carlos Janes	Frank L. Packard
Arthur Schnitzler	Donald Keyhoe	Frank V. Webster
Atticus	Dorothy Kilner	Frederic Stewart Isham
B.H. Baden-Powell	Dougan Clark	Frederick Trevor Hill
B. M. Bower	Douglas Fairbanks	Frederick Winslow Taylor
B. C. Chatterjee	E. Nesbit	Friedrich Kerst
Baroness Emmuska Orczy	E.P.Roe	Friedrich Nietzsche
Baroness Orczy	E. Phillips Oppenheim	Fyodor Dostoyevsky
Basil King	Earl Barnes	G.A. Henty
Bayard Taylor	Edgar Rice Burroughs	G.K. Chesterton
Ben Macomber	Edith Van Dyne	Gabrielle E. Jackson
Bertha Muzzy Bower	Edith Wharton	Garrett P. Serviss
Bjornstjerne Bjornson	Edward Everett Hale	Gaston Leroux
Booth Tarkington	Edward J. O'Biren	George A. Warren
Boyd Cable	Edward S. Ellis	George Ade
Bram Stoker	Edwin L. Arnold	Geroge Bernard Shaw
C. Collodi	Eleanor Atkins	George Durston
C. E. Orr	Eliot Gregory	George Ebers

George Eliot
George Gissing
George MacDonald
George Meredith
George Orwell
George Sylvester Viereck
George Tucker
George W. Cable
George Wharton James
Gertrude Atherton
Gordon Casserly
Grace E. King
Grace Gallatin
Grace Greenwood
Grant Allen
Guillermo A. Sherwell
Gulielma Zollinger
Gustav Flaubert
H. A. Cody
H. B. Irving
H.C. Bailey
H. G. Wells
H. H. Munro
H. Irving Hancock
H. Rider Haggard
H. W. C. Davis
Haldeman Julius
Hall Caine
Hamilton Wright Mabie
Hans Christian Andersen
Harold Avery
Harold McGrath
Harriet Beecher Stowe
Harry Castlemon
Harry Coghill
Harry Houidini
Hayden Carruth
Helent Hunt Jackson
Helen Nicolay
Hendrik Conscience
Hendy David Thoreau
Henri Barbusse
Henrik Ibsen
Henry Adams
Henry Ford
Henry Frost
Henry James
Henry Jones Ford
Henry Seton Merriman
Henry W Longfellow
Herbert A. Giles

Herbert Carter
Herbert N. Casson
Herman Hesse
Hildegard G. Frey
Homer
Honore De Balzac
Horace B. Day
Horace Walpole
Horatio Alger Jr.
Howard Pyle
Howard R. Garis
Hugh Lofting
Hugh Walpole
Humphry Ward
Ian Maclaren
Inez Haynes Gillmore
Irving Bacheller
Isabel Hornibrook
Israel Abrahams
Ivan Turgenev
J.G.Austin
J. Henri Fabre
J. M. Barrie
J. Macdonald Oxley
J. S. Fletcher
J. S. Knowles
J. Storer Clouston
Jack London
Jacob Abbott
James Allen
James Andrews
James Baldwin
James Branch Cabell
James DeMille
James Joyce
James Lane Allen
James Lane Allen
James Oliver Curwood
James Oppenheim
James Otis
James R. Driscoll
Jane Austen
Jane L. Stewart
Janet Aldridge
Jens Peter Jacobsen
Jerome K. Jerome
John Burroughs
John Cournos
John F. Kennedy
John Gay
John Glasworthy

John Habberton
John Joy Bell
John Kendrick Bangs
John Milton
John Philip Sousa
Jonas Lauritz Idemil Lie
Jonathan Swift
Joseph A. Altsheler
Joseph Carey
Joseph Conrad
Joseph E. Badger Jr
Joseph Hergesheimer
Joseph Jacobs
Jules Vernes
Julian Hawthrone
Julie A Lippmann
Justin Huntly McCarthy
Kakuzo Okakura
Kenneth Grahame
Kenneth McGaffey
Kate Langley Bosher
Kate Langley Bosher
Katherine Cecil Thurston
Katherine Stokes
L. A. Abbot
L. T. Meade
L. Frank Baum
Latta Griswold
Laura Dent Crane
Laura Lee Hope
Laurence Housman
Lawrence Beasley
Leo Tolstoy
Leonid Andreyev
Lewis Carroll
Lewis Sperry Chafer
Lilian Bell
Lloyd Osbourne
Louis Hughes
Louis Tracy
Louisa May Alcott
Lucy Fitch Perkins
Lucy Maud Montgomery
Luther Benson
Lydia Miller Middleton
Lyndon Orr
M. Corvus
M. H. Adams
Margaret E. Sangster
Margret Howth
Margaret Vandercook

Margret Penrose
Maria Edgeworth
Maria Thompson Daviess
Mariano Azuela
Marion Polk Angellotti
Mark Overton
Mark Twain
Mary Austin
Mary Catherine Crowley
Mary Cole
Mary Hastings Bradley
Mary Roberts Rinehart
Mary Rowlandson
M. Wollstonecraft Shelley
Maud Lindsay
Max Beerbohm
Myra Kelly
Nathaniel Hawthrone
Nicolo Machiavelli
O. F. Walton
Oscar Wilde
Owen Johnson
P.G. Wodehouse
Paul and Mabel Thorne
Paul G. Tomlinson
Paul Severing
Percy Brebner
Peter B. Kyne
Plato
R. Derby Holmes
R. L. Stevenson
R. S. Ball
Rabindranath Tagore
Rahul Alvares
Ralph Bonehill
Ralph Henry Barbour
Ralph Victor
Ralph Waldo Emmerson
Rene Descartes
Rex Beach
Rex E. Beach
Richard Harding Davis
Richard Jefferies
Richard Le Gallienne
Robert Barr
Robert Frost
Robert Gordon Anderson
Robert L. Drake
Robert Lansing
Robert Lynd
Robert Michael Ballantyne

Robert W. Chambers
Rosa Nouchette Carey
Rudyard Kipling
Samuel B. Allison
Samuel Hopkins Adams
Sarah Bernhardt
Sarah C. Hallowell
Selma Lagerlof
Sherwood Anderson
Sigmund Freud
Standish O'Grady
Stanley Weyman
Stella Benson
Stella M. Francis
Stephen Crane
Stewart Edward White
Stijn Streuvels
Swami Abhedananda
Swami Parmananda
T. S. Ackland
T. S. Arthur
The Princess Der Ling
Thomas A. Janvier
Thomas A Kempis
Thomas Anderton
Thomas Bailey Aldrich
Thomas Bulfinch
Thomas De Quincey
Thomas Dixon
Thomas H. Huxley
Thomas Hardy
Thomas More
Thornton W. Burgess
U. S. Grant
Valentine Williams
Various Authors
Vaughan Kester
Victor Appleton
Victoria Cross
Virginia Woolf
Wadsworth Camp
Walter Camp
Walter Scott
Washington Irving
Wilbur Lawton
Wilkie Collins
Willa Cather
Willard F. Baker
William Dean Howells
William le Queux
W. Makepeace Thackeray

William W. Walter
William Shakespeare
Winston Churchill
Yei Theodora Ozaki
Yogi Ramacharaka
Young E. Allison
Zane Grey

Lightning Source UK Ltd.
Milton Keynes UK
22 January 2010

148959UK00001B/144/A

9 781421 824642